WITHDRAWN

MUSIC

IN THE

CLASSROOM

For if the trumpet give an uncertain
sound, who shall prepare himself to
the battle?

I Corinthians, xiv, 8

MUSIC
IN THE
CLASSROOM

by

Bernarr Rainbow

SECOND EDITION

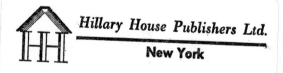

Hillary House Publishers Ltd.

New York

HEINEMANN
LONDON

Heinemann Educational Books Ltd
LONDON MELBOURNE EDINBURGH TORONTO
SINGAPORE JOHANNESBURG AUCKLAND IBADAN
NAIROBI HONG KONG NEW DELHI

ISBN 0 435 81746 9

Published by
Heinemann Educational Books Ltd
48 Charles Street, London W1X 8AH

Printed in Great Britain by
Morrison and Gibb Ltd., London and Edinburgh

Contents

Chapter		Page
1	MUSIC AND TEACHING *The teacher's attitude—Music and the Curriculum—The scope of school music*	1
2	MUSIC AND CHILDREN *Teaching children to listen—Talking about music—Music and the Adolescent*	7
3	CHORAL MUSIC *Possibilities and needs—Class management for singing—The song library—The singing lesson—Two-part singing*	15
4	TEACHING NOTATION *Rhythm—Pitch—Clefs—Dotted notes—Rests—Time signatures—Key signatures—Examinations*	27
5	TEACHING SINGING *Breathing—Breath control—Vocal registers—Tone production—The adolescent voice—Diction—Line and phrasing—Teaching a new song—School choir festivals—Choosing songs—'Groaners'*	45
6	INSTRUMENTAL MUSIC *Percussion work—Unpitched percussion—pitched percussion—Creative work—Writing for percussion—Melody writing—Instrumental tuition—The School Orchestra and Band*	64
7	THE SCHOOL, AND MUSIC TODAY *The example of the art lesson—Music-making in a new idiom*	81
8	OTHER MUSICAL ACTIVITIES *Listening to music—Presentation of recorded music—Television and radio lessons—Correlation with other subjects Private recordings—House music competitions—Combined school festivals—Concerts for schools*	91
9	SOME GENERAL CONSIDERATIONS *Integrated music-teaching—The teacher and his class—Conclusion*	100

CONTENTS

APPENDIX

I   *Some useful books*   107
II   *Extract from a Report on the Training of Teachers in France*   110
III   *Extract from a Report on Aids in Music Education*   111
IV   *The French Rhythm-names*   113

INDEX   115

Preface to the Second Edition

During the fourteen years which have passed since this book first appeared school music has undergone something of a revolution. New trends and techniques introduced in recent years have transformed the music lesson by underlining a creative approach and by encouraging the making of music by the children themselves. The emphasis in modern music-teaching is upon learning by doing.

To take account of such substantial changes in attitude has called for equally substantial revision in this new edition, and the range of the book has also been enlarged by the addition of new chapters dealing with creative work, instrumental work, and the introduction of music in a contemporary idiom. At the same time the opportunity has been taken to extend the treatment of points of class management and control. Experience has shown that it is insecurity in these areas of their work that minimizes the effectiveness of many young teachers' initial efforts in the classroom.

B. R.

January 1971

Acknowledgements

Thanks are due to the following authors, or their representatives, and publishers for permission to quote copyright material: Novello & Company Ltd, extract from Harold Greenhill's song 'Time, you old gipsy-man'; United Nations Educational, Scientific and Cultural Organization, two extracts from *Music in Education* (distributed in the United Kingdom by H.M.S.O.); Universal Edition (London) Ltd, for the extract from Bernard Rand's *Sound Patterns I*.

1. Music and Teaching

When a good teacher of music leaves a school, it is by no means unusual for the music in that school to collapse very soon after his departure. No other subject in the curriculum depends so heavily for its well-being and status upon the personal quality of the individual teacher concerned.

In the chapters that follow, various aspects of school music, and various methods of presenting the subject in schools will be considered in turn. But every one of the tried teaching devices outlined in these pages really depends for its success upon the attitude of the teacher to his class. A dull teacher may employ exactly the same material as an alert teacher; and yet the result will be disappointing. Our first consideration, then, must be with the teacher's attitude.

For music teaching to be successful it must be enjoyed. The teacher must be able to infect his pupils with his own enthusiasm for music. It is not enough for him to like music himself; he must be able to project that liking. For instance, it is possible to love music genuinely, and yet to appear bored while listening to it. The good music teacher never makes that mistake in the classroom. He may well have heard a particular recording a thousand times before; but when he next plays it to his pupils, he knows that he must be seen to be listening to it as if it were fresh from the composer's pen. When he introduces the school choir to a work which he knows inside out, he must be able to convince the singers that he and they are about to launch upon a new and delightful experience together. Even when he teaches the distinction between a crotchet and a quaver, he must be able to make the matter seem of vital importance to him. For, if he does not seem to care, why should the class?

This does not mean that the teacher is required either to 'gush', or to be dishonest—to put on an act. The situation is to some extent paradoxical, in that provided the teacher *remembers* to keep alert, his pupils' response will automatically stimulate genuine freshness in his teaching. Good teaching re-charges the teacher's batteries, as it were. In front of a class that he is teaching well, the teacher finds himself at the receiving end of a surge of energy: the class gives back to him as he gives to them.

To be a good musician yourself is not enough. Beethoven, with his short temper, dominating attitude, impatience, and scorn for the unmusical, would clearly have been a disastrous failure in the classroom. Haydn, on the other hand, judging by accounts of his geniality, sincerity, sense of humour, and the good relations which he established with his players at Eszterháza, would almost certainly have made a fine teacher. Other qualities than musicianship are called for in the teacher: qualities without which a man's musical gifts will be unable to touch his pupils.

To begin with, the teacher must learn to see through the child's eyes and hear with his ears. Music is only 'good' or 'bad' within a context. And what is 'good' in the Festival Hall is not necessarily 'good' in the classroom. Many young teachers are so absorbed by their own recent musical discoveries, by the newly clarified mysteries of musical form and history gleaned during their own training, that they are bursting to share them with the first children they can lay hands on. Inevitably, they are disappointed at the result. They have forgotten that children can respond only so far as their past musical experience allows. Instead of trotting out 'imposing' jargon, and plastering the board with technicalities such as *Binary Form*, or *Fugal Exposition*, the young teacher should ask himself what real value the introduction of those terms, at that particular point, has for the advancement of the child's musical sympathy and understanding. This is not to say that technical terms should not be used, in due course and in their appropriate context. Music has its own vocabulary, like any other serious subject.

Before trying to interest children in some aspect of music which happens to appeal to him personally, the teacher should try to think back to his own musical responses at their age. He should try to recall the type of thing which attracted him then, and so 'tune in' to the child's wavelength. Often enough, if he is honest with himself, the teacher will find that he is quite ashamed of some of the music which he enjoyed at an early age. But, recovering from that reaction, he will realize that taste is something which develops with experience; and will thus have stumbled upon an important fact about children which every musician ought to appreciate—namely, that children can enjoy music of quite different kinds at different levels in a way that adults may find strange. A youngster can listen to 'pops' and 'classics' with equal enjoyment. He can enjoy both, without at all feeling them to be mutually contradictory. The same boy who played the clarinet in a perhaps somewhat staid orchestral rehearsal can often be found slamming away in a school 'pop' group almost immediately afterwards. One thing does not automatically exclude the other—as some might suppose.

The wise teacher is therefore careful not to adopt a snobbish attitude towards music—either to music performed in the classroom or to the music which children enjoy at home. In this way, he will avoid encouraging the partisan attitude which can easily arise where older pupils, especially, are concerned. He should not hide from his pupils that he, too, can look on music light-heartedly, and that he can find pleasure in some of its less serious forms, as well as in its masterpieces.

A common failing in early attempts at music teaching appears to arise from the teacher's own subconscious sense of insecurity. In an attempt to overcome this feeling, he sets out to impress the class by a display of his own superior knowledge. Whatever the consolation for the teacher himself, this approach has a most unfortunate effect upon his class.

Never feel it beneath your dignity to adjust yourself to the level of the children you are teaching. To do so is quite different from patronizing them, or talking down to them. When you have estimated the intellectual level of a group of children, begin your work at that level, setting out to develop a relaxed, chatty, atmosphere. If your lesson is well planned, it will then prove possible to make the lesson appear spontaneous and natural. You can thus strengthen your contact and easy relationship with the children in a way that would be quite impossible were a superior, pontifical manner to be adopted. Some few teachers, alas, appear quite unable to unbend. Both they and their classes suffer accordingly.

MUSIC AND THE CURRICULUM

One of the less obvious tasks of the music teacher in a secondary school is to fight for the recognition of his subject as an equal in the school curriculum. Because music was a comparative latecomer to the modern scheme of secondary education, it still tends to be looked upon by the unprogressive as an educational frill.

The music teacher must resist any attempt to treat his subject as special or peculiar, and do all he can to see that it occupies a normal place and plays an integral part in the work of the school. There is still a tendency for teachers of other subjects in secondary schools to look on music as an 'extra'. Even those of them who value school music at all are prone to see it as providing a light relief to other more serious matters—such as their own subjects. This view is perhaps more common in grammar schools, where music is sometimes elbowed out of existence by the examination bogey.

Anyone who has watched children wrestling with the problems presented by serious musical participation will be in a position to see that, aesthetic considerations apart, the mental exercise involved in musical activity is every bit as demanding and valuable as that presented by other 'more orthodox' activities. The children are at grips with another language. But the music teacher may not find his colleagues—even his headmaster—aware of this. They, presumably, are obliged to base their estimate upon an indifferent musical experience in their own schooldays.

Because of this common failure to discern the educational value of school music, the young teacher may find that in his school the subject is allotted only a single weekly period on the time-table. A weekly singing-lesson is still standard fare in some schools. Indeed, in a few of them, that single period has to be shared by two or three classes who are herded together into the hall for what amounts to a glorified sing-song.

Such provision is simply not good enough. Every class should have its own time for music every week. Two periods should be the minimum time allowed, at least until the third year in the secondary school. To attempt to teach the elements of musical awareness to a horde of ninety or so uninstructed children at a time is a hopeless task. Any head teacher who allows this to happen must be desperately unaware of musical values himself.

If it is your serious intention to teach children to love and understand music, you will not regard the singing class as the limit of musical experience. There are so many things still to be achieved. The singing of a few songs by rote is an unworthy goal.

THE SCOPE OF SCHOOL MUSIC

Stated in its simplest terms, the ideal music course will provide opportunities for three main fields of activity: singing and instrumental music—with a creative element incorporated; the consequent development of the use of notation; and 'guided' listening. In every school today one or more of those activities holds a place. But it is not always possible to find all three being developed consistently; and still less so to find all of them recognized as forming essential and complementary elements in the music course.

This is, perhaps, because the potential field of school music has grown so wide nowadays that it is easy for the teacher to lose his sense of direction. So many different aspects of the subject beckon, that he can easily find himself developing one activity at the expense of another, equally vital one. When this sort of thing happens, it usually means that the teacher has begun to work keenly at one particular part of his task without first asking himself what his *whole* task is to be.

Now, if the content of the ideal music course suggested above is examined, and a reason is supplied for the inclusion of each of its three elements, the purpose of music teaching can be stated in the following terms:

The ideal music course will help children to become
 (i) musically articulate;
 (ii) musically literate;
 (iii) musically responsive.

Regarded in that light, the relationship between the three elements present becomes clearer, and the fact that each complements the others is revealed.

The teacher who keeps sight of this three-fold purpose in his work will be less likely to find himself devoting most of his time and energy to the development of one aspect of music at the expense of the rest.

He will encourage performance, not just because it allows him to mount an imposing choral display when an audience assembles in the school, but because he realizes that children's first real approach to music comes from the music which they make themselves. After they have begun to develop some skill in music-making, they are more ready to learn about notes, or to listen to others performing.

He will introduce children to the use of musical notation, not because it provides a nice subject for the setting of written tests, or adds a rather impressively 'academic' element to his syllabus, but because growing understanding of notation increases his pupils' opportunity to make music, as well as helping them in their listening.

He will provide occasions for children to listen to music, not because the activity passes the time pleasantly in the classroom, but because children need help in realizing that hearing and listening are not at all the same thing, and call for different mental processes.

Above all, he will remember that music exists to give pleasure, and must be taught with that end in view. He will not, however, overlook the fact that a prime source of pleasure lies in achievement—and that children should not be deprived of challenging opportunities, both in the physical disciplines of performance and in the intellectual exercise that the creation of music, the interpretation of notation and active listening all afford.

Once the teacher has framed and begun to act upon a policy of this kind, he will find that the music in his school acquires a new sense of purpose. If he is able, in addition, to establish good relations with his pupils, he will discover that their response to his teaching soon begins to bring music to life there.

2. *Music and Children*

For many schools singing is the standard form of musical activity. But this need not, as it often does, prevent the teacher from encouraging the children to realize that the matter in hand is music. They should have copies of the music they sing and should be shown how to read it. Remember that they can learn not only by trying to read a tune that they don't know, but quite as much by associating the 'shape' of a known tune with its appearance in the symbols of musical notation.

Begin to tackle the problems of perception even with the youngest by demonstrating the way in which the rise and fall of a melody can be shown pictorially. The National Anthem, even for those without any previous musical knowledge, can be recognized as conforming with this outline, which may be drawn in 'blocks' on the board with the edge of a piece of chalk:

Can be so recognized, that is, by all those who agree with what we so readily accept as 'rise' and 'fall' in musical parlance. The teacher will do well, however, to realize that a child with little musical experience may not have accepted this convention. For that is all that it is. Notes do not, of course, rise and fall physically; some vibrate faster, that is all. And to inexperienced children different notes do not automatically suggest variations in height. But most children accept this convention easily enough even before going to school at all. And the fact that they have since often heard the expression 'up the scale' or 'down the scale' has emphasized the terms and led to their automatic acceptance.

Wrong notes in singing can be clearly identified and the mistake explained when a picture of the tune is put on the board. How often there is confusion with an ending of this kind:

7

Is it this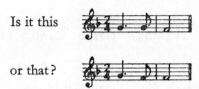

or that?

Put up your diagram of the correct version: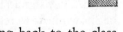

and then sing both the right and the wrong back to the class. They will unhesitatingly tell you which is correct.

Diagrams which set out the 'shape' of tunes should be frequently used in the classroom. Whenever a phrase of a melody is being discussed, whether it is part of music to be sung or a significant figure in music to be listened to, the teacher is doubling the effectiveness of what he says by making visual reference in a quick blackboard sketch to the line of the music.

Schubert's 'Who is Sylvia?' begins like this:

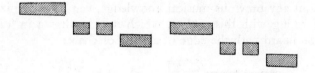

At once a new feature of the music is made clear. The second phrase repeats the first, but lower down. The children are at grips with the very nature of the music. Now most of us could sing this song a dozen times without consciously noticing what the eye detects at once. And this has a considerable bearing on the problems of talking to children about music, as well as helping them to learn to read notation.

It is a first step towards getting the child to *listen*. Many children come from homes where the radio is allowed to play for hours on end with no one giving any real attention to what is coming from the speaker. They don't listen—they overhear. You have only to try to recall the details of the pattern on your bedroom wallpaper to realize just how easy it is to stop noticing something which is always with you. In many homes the music broadcast provides nothing more than a vague background to conversation and general domestic activity. It is a kind of audible wallpaper which no one notices any more. There is a danger that this will become the child's attitude to all music. The widespread casual use of transistor radios underlines the danger. The teacher who thinks about all this realizes that most of his pupils will have to learn to listen actively, and not just hear, before anything else can be done.

At first, they will learn about music best by performing it. Later, in schools where music is sufficiently developed to introduce children to creative work, they will learn through their own early efforts to 'compose'. Both stages are desirable to prepare children to meet the adult fare of the concert hall. And when that state is reached, the teacher must choose their listening material carefully, and not allow himself to talk too much.

TALKING ABOUT MUSIC

Children are easily misled about music as about other things. Many children believe that all music is 'about' something. This is perhaps because the old way of dealing with that dangerous thing called 'musical appreciation' was to select pieces of music in which the composer deliberately set out to describe something —programme music, with clearly defined intention and with titles that made the subject-matter abundantly plain. In such a case any teacher with imagination and the power to express himself felt (at last!) on firm ground. He could explore the implications of the title for the bulk of the lesson and then allow the music to do its best to paraphrase what he had said during the time that was left. It was all so dangerously easy. And the children appeared to enjoy it too. They responded to the enthusiasm with which the teacher described the scene for them. They always enjoy a story well told. And they felt able to follow the music when it was played. I have done this sort of thing too, and seen a class of small boys listening to the storm in *William Tell* with their coat collars turned up to keep out the rain.

By all means let your classes hear and enjoy programme music. But tackle the problem of listening to absolute music as well. This is a different, and in many ways a much more difficult, matter. But remember that if a child's experience in 'guided'

M.I.C.—2

listening is limited to music which is descriptive, there is a very real danger of him being encouraged to believe that this is true of all music. As a result, many of his later attempts to listen for himself will be fruitless. He will be trying to discover events and situations which are not there, in music which is not attempting to describe anything at all. And after all, by far the greater part of music is not descriptive. It is just music.

When first introducing 'absolute' music as listening material you will be wise to limit your comments to points such as rhythmic structures (perhaps based on dance-rhythms), phrase-balance and cadence, sequence, simple formal structures, key-relationship, and the like. In dealing with these avoid using technical terms for their own sake—express yourself in everyday language. Children will be helped to appreciate points of melodic interest if a 'diagram' of the shape of a tune is shown pictorially on the blackboard.

Most music lovers who have studied musical works with a score before them know how often points of construction which the ear does not detect at a first hearing are revealed by the eye—because the eye is able to dwell on the score for much longer than it takes for the passage in question to be performed. This should emphasize the value of a method which enables a teacher to present children with a 'picture' of a tune. It should give a clue as to the way in which older children with limited experience in music can begin to investigate, for instance, the construction of melodies, and later follow more extended and elaborate music. Show them that Beethoven's Fifth Symphony begins like this:

and they can follow the adventures of that shape in what comes next.

The older children in a secondary school will respond to this sort of thing. They can also be introduced to the mysteries of symphonic development with the aid of this pictorial approach. Haydn's 'London' Symphony, for instance, has a subject which contains a readily recognizable figure from which the whole of the development section grows:

A picture of this germinating figure

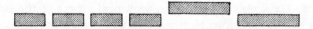

will give the class something tangible to reckon with. With the
eye to help it, the ear has much more chance of following this
little musical pattern when Haydn begins to juggle with it. With
the diagram before them, the class can identify the 'shape' as it
passes from top to bottom of the orchestra and from one
instrument to another.

Because they have not realized this possibility, and since most
of their pupils cannot read an orchestral score—even if copies
were available—many young teachers never attempt to interest
their classes in the 'nature' of music. Yet, if they are to be
'educated' in any sense of the word, the senior pupils in a secondary
school should certainly be introduced to an approach more adult
than the superficial method of pretending that music is just a
peculiar way of telling stories, or painting 'mood pictures'.

MUSIC AND THE ADOLESCENT

Adolescence presents problems to any teacher; with a subject
such as music, those problems are often intensified. Older boys,
in particular, naturally want to cast off any activity which seems
to be 'kids' stuff', or 'only for girls'. Merely to insist on continuing
the pattern of lesson more usual in the lower school will only
strengthen the adolescent's determination to resist. If music is to
continue in the upper secondary school, it must acquire a new
image.

To abandon music with the adolescent pupil is not only a
token of defeat; it will create a vicious circle—because the lower
classes in the school then come to look on their music as 'something to grow out of'. Ways must be found to avoid this danger
by injecting new life into music teaching in the upper secondary
school. Here are some suggestions. Some of them are directed

principally towards attracting the older boy—his attitude towards music is often more aggressively unfavourable than the girl's, because he has experienced that upsetting thing, the breaking voice.

Most youngsters are interested in finding out 'How things work'. That interest can be applied to music readily enough by means of a simple study of the acoustical aspect of the subject. Some simple experiments, conducted with the co-operation of the physics department, to show the way in which the pitch of a stretched string varies according to its length and tension would make an obvious starting-point. A subsequent examination of the properties of a vibrating column of air could lead to direct application of the findings of both experiments to the whole range of orchestral instruments. Differences of tone-colour can be most absorbingly demonstrated on an oscilloscope. A tape-recorder capable of playing at different speeds can be made the basis of further experiments, even of some initial 'electronic' music—by dubbing recordings of classroom music-making at one speed on to subsequent recordings at another. Even the tuning-fork can be used imaginatively to illustrate some of the properties of sound. For the teacher with ideas, there is no shortage of simple textbooks on acoustics to help in preparing some interesting work in this field. Steer clear of the drumming-in of formulae; satisfy yourself with helping the class to find out things about sound which are new to them.

Another and perhaps more challenging line of approach is to tackle the matter of the changing voice itself. It is no longer believed that a boy's voice should be completely rested after it has 'broken'. Indeed, it is realized that most treble voices do not 'break' at all. Provided that a young boy has been encouraged to use his treble voice properly, and is not allowed, or coerced—by repeated injunctions to 'Sing Up' while the voice change is taking place—to force his vocal apparatus, it is far more likely that his voice will undergo a gradual change. What usually happens is that the treble voice begins to lose the bottom notes of its range while the top notes are still useable and very strong. As the bottom notes weaken successively, a new range of notes in the baritone compass becomes available.

There is absolutely no harm in using those new notes if they are employed carefully, and so long as the boy does not strain for others beyond his limits at the time. If a boy is to rest his voice completely at this stage, as used to be argued, then he will not be able to raise his voice as a supporter at a football match, or in the street. No one will concede that he is likely to refrain in that way, or that the thousands who have successfully negotiated this same vocal change did so before him.

Let these boys sing with their new baritone voices. They may react unfavourably to the suggestion at first, but they will get over it if handled well. You cannot force them to sing; but you can interest them in the possibility of this novel idea—especially if you will adjust your own ideas as to the music which they should perform. If you expect them to make their first attempts by singing an aria, you will naturally be disappointed. Something that calls for guitar accompaniment and suggests a cowpuncher is more likely to succeed. The harmonic simplicity of many of the songs of a type that will interest young baritones of this age makes the production of a simple vocal harmonization particularly straightforward for the teacher to devise at a later stage. Bass parts of the I, IV, V, type—often simple *ostinati*—are common in such ditties. They make a good starting-point for young baritones when singing in parts is first introduced.

Sooner or later in this type of activity the problem of notating the songs must crop up. Some of those who *can* sing at this age will find themselves less competent than they would like at reading their parts. Sol-fa is not likely to appeal to them as an approach device. Sol-fa works only if the syllables can be interpreted as second nature; and that facility comes only after long practice. With older 'beginners', try codifying simple tunes in figures. The bass part of the National Anthem, for instance, makes sense more readily to the adolescent beginner in this form:

Figuring of this type should be pencilled in on the copies of the music employed.

In the Grammar and Comprehensive schools, those boys who remain on till the age of eighteen or nineteen will later be able to take part in fully fledged choral works from the ordinary repertoire. It is therefore desirable that they should begin to get the feel of singing a part as soon as their voices allow. It is equally desirable, however, that those boys who are due to leave school before that age is reached should be introduced to the use of their 'baritone' voices. The early age of puberty in these days makes singing possible again before the lower school-leaving age is reached.

Instrumental music-making offers another field for the teenage pupil. By the time that children who have grown accustomed to using instruments in the classroom reach the upper school, they will be ready to learn to make their own arrangements and even to compose their own pieces. As long as the type of music embarked upon is sufficiently close to their own musical experience, even the most unpromising pupils can become interested in this work. Methods of developing this facility are discussed in the chapter on Instrumental Music which appears later in this book. Those pupils who have not acquired the necessary experience in the lower school can be introduced to the techniques at this stage. Another type of creative instrumental activity especially suitable for the development of a new attitude toward the music lesson in the upper secondary school is discussed in Chapter Seven: 'The School, and Music Today'.

3. Choral Music

Every school should have its choir. It should be as great a privilege to belong to the school choir as to belong to any of the school teams. The children should have this pointed out to them as often as is necessary, preferably by the headmaster. It should meet, like the teams, which are also drawn from different parts of the school, out of school hours. After lunch is quite a good time now that most children have their midday meal at school.

It should not be a tiny handpicked affair which exists only to perform on special occasions when the Mayor and Governors are present, but one which admits as many as can pass a few simple vocal and aural tests. Its purpose should be to give those children opportunities of a musical experience quite beyond the attainments of ordinary class-singing; to let the younger children feel the thrill of performing with a large body including more experienced singers, and to allow the older ones to savour the privileges and responsibilities of leadership.

In handling the school choir the music teacher must set himself and them high standards. He should encourage its members to realize that he is inviting them to join with him in making music together, letting them feel that they are essential to the success of the activity. Consequently he will endeavour in his choir practices to produce an atmosphere and attitude quite different from that of the ordinary classroom.

Every class seems to have its 'groaners' who sing on one note whatever the tune. Freed from the limitations that these impose, both teacher and children can, in the work of the school choir, rise to heights which are never likely to be attained in ordinary class work. And both parties quickly appreciate this.

Time is the snag. But an enthusiastic music teacher—and he is the only one to succeed—will soon realize that some of his most effective work is done outside the ordinary time-table. In order to draw together children whose age-range compels them to work in different classes and to entirely different time-tables, it is often essential for the music teacher to be prepared to devote a lot of his own time to the organization and rehearsal of voluntary groups. Choir, recorder ensemble, orchestra, band, a music club to listen to records and arrange little recitals, as well as rehearsals for plays and concerts, all depend for their existence on the amount of time the teacher is prepared to invest in them.

When planning a school time-table it is sometimes possible to arrange an 'Activities' period when singers can go to their choir practice while others go to crafts, gardening, puppetry and the like. It is worth discussing this possibility with your colleagues and headmaster.

POSSIBILITIES AND NEEDS

Headmasters are often said to be unhelpful where music is concerned and the subject dubbed a Cinderella in many schools. But there are very few headmasters who will not give support to an activity which 'shows results'.

Make it one of your aims to present a school concert or a performance by the school choir which can be enjoyed by your audience. Remember that a first essential of the public performance of music is that it should give pleasure. Choose items which are within the power of your performers. Without pandering to your audience, see that the programme will please. Perhaps your headmaster's previous experience of school performances has been limited to occasions when the audience sat miserably on the edge of the seat waiting for something to go wrong.

The school choir is, incidentally, a shop-window for the school's music. If there are signs that the music in his school is beginning to flourish and that the school's reputation is likely to be enhanced by it, no headmaster will withhold support for new ideas you may wish to introduce. But do not use the choir to display children who have been drilled against their will like performing animals, or as a mere weapon in school politics. The activity itself should be its own reward.

The young teacher will be wise to make it his policy to assess the potential of the material at his disposal, and determine to reach the best standard within those limits as a first aim. If the piano is bad, see that it is at least properly tuned and maintained. If there are no gramophone records, be prepared at first to borrow from the local library, or to buy and lend your own.

If your record-player gives better reproduction than the one at school, bring it and use it instead.

Patience is needed in the early stages. But once your pupils begin to respond, once the school choir is able to put on something enjoyable, then you can begin to ask for the improvements that you know are needed. And if you are wise enough not to ask for everything at once, you can hope to get what you want. You will find it helpful in deciding where your priorities lie to consult some of the publications dealing with accommodation and equipment for music in schools: *Music in Schools*, 2nd edition, (H.M.S.O.), *A Guide to the Purchase and Care of Musical Instruments*, (Schools Music Association), and the chapter on *Planning a Music Department* in *The Handbook for Music Teachers* (Novello).

CLASS MANAGEMENT FOR SINGING

Muddle, the result usually of inadequate preparation, is too frequently a feature of the music lesson and the choir practice. If you are rehearsing a song which calls for piano accompaniment, see that your piano is in such a position that you can see all your singers as you play for them. An upright piano may look tidier with its back to the wall, but the caretaker who plants it there will not know that this is quite the worst position for class use. Many teachers find it best to acquire the ability to play standing up facing the class, with the music lying flat on the piano lid. The children can then be seen without a barrier between. A grand piano probably provides the best type of instrument for the teacher who needs to see his class while he plays, but few schools possess one and this kind is not essential.

Above all, the teacher of class-singing must acquire facility in playing song accompaniments without gluing his eyes to the music. His playing must be so assured that *most* of his attention is free to control the class and assess their singing. Indifferent singing by school-children is often due to the fact that their teacher has been so busily occupied playing the right notes in accompanying them that he has not listened critically to their efforts at all. If you cannot do this sort of thing easily, do not attempt to accompany songs until your playing has improved with further practice.

Learn to make a 'skeleton' accompaniment for rehearsal purposes—one that provides only the essential harmonies at pivot points and cadences, leaving the singers unsupported elsewhere. Then you can concentrate on what your singers are doing; and they will learn self-assurance at the same time. Many teachers are prone to over-use the piano in their singing lessons, by playing too often, too much, and too loud.

Folksongs should be sung unaccompanied, or with the simplest accompaniments, for instance on a guitar. The ability to play this instrument is a resource worth developing. It makes a welcome relief to the piano, is portable, and can be played facing the class—even while moving around among them. Its popularity with young people today is a consideration not to be overlooked in schools. Remember, too, that once they have been given opportunities to try their hand at creative writing, children can produce worthwhile instrumental accompaniments of their own to simple songs of this kind. The topic is discussed in Chapter Six.

Arrange the singers sensibly. Not in a long line so that their voices do not 'add up'; not in a heap so that you cannot see and control them. Let them stand comfortably, and remember that they should not be kept standing unnecessarily or for too long at a time. Seats are essential. No one can sing properly squatting on the floor. If you cannot avoid working in the school hall, ask for sufficient seats to accommodate a class there. Forms will do.

A great deal of a singing period—the learning of a new song for instance—can be carried out with the class sitting down. It is then possible to secure a refreshing change of atmosphere by letting the children stand to try through what they have learned. Remember too that, particularly with boys, forcing the voice is less likely when the singers are seated. Distinguish sharply between sitting and lounging. Whether sitting or standing, the children should be in loose easy positions free from muscular tension.

THE SONG LIBRARY

Copies of music should be distributed methodically. Inefficiency in this respect makes a gap in the lesson and destroys any feeling of enthusiasm which you may have been able to build up. Perhaps a monitor system with one child from a group of six or eight made responsible for distribution and collection works best. Keep your music tidily. It pays to file each set of copies separately in an indexed box. The extra cost is more than justified by the increased life of the copies. And you can find things quickly when you need them.

Check all copies regularly for tears and missing pages, and make sure that copies are returned after use with the covers closed. Encourage the children to handle music with respect, if only for their own future convenience. Music should be held like a book, not twisted back on itself. Children, like adults, hate using torn copies, and much time can be wasted on complaints about missing pages.

Decide on the maximum amount of music you are likely to need during each period and have all the copies available before the lesson begins. It is better to have too much at hand than to interrupt the flow of your work while a search goes on for further copies.

You may find on arriving at the school where you are to teach that there are no music copies available. Many schools seem, regrettably, to work only from duplicated copies of the words of songs. In such a case you will have twice as much material if you buy copies on the basis of one shared by two children. This sharing of copies has much to commend it, besides the saving involved. A good collection of songs published in one volume with a 'melody only' edition for the children is probably the best answer in a case like this.

Once copies are provided, see that the children learn to make full use of them. Do not attempt to explain the significance of all the musical symbols. Wait until these arise in turn in your course of work. But help them to understand the layout of the score—especially when the accompaniment is included in their copies—and explain the marks of expression. At first their attention will tend to be limited to the *words* of the songs. Encourage them to gain familiarity with notation by following the notes and omitting the words, and let them point to each note as they sing or as you play over a tune.

To begin with, they may only be able to see the general trend of rise and fall, but this is an important step, and as their classwork in notation proceeds, they will gain more confidence and ability. Eventually the time taken to learn a new song will be very considerably curtailed, and the path opened for regular part-singing.

One way of giving every child a daily opportunity of meeting and growing familiar with musical notation is to see that the hymn book used for daily assembly includes the melody of the hymns. Many hymn books are published with a 'melody only' edition.

THE SINGING LESSON

Never begin a lesson by trying to teach a new song. Always give the children an opportunity first of singing something they are familiar with and which they can enjoy. Then you can settle down to the task of teaching something new with a better chance of success.

Avoid a temptation to dwell too long on one task. Too many attempts at correcting an error in singing will only tire and bore the children. The law of diminishing returns applies here. This does not mean that difficulties should be avoided and mistakes left uncorrected. The teacher should always be aware of the reactions of his class and should learn to judge just when further insistence is going to produce less work. A change of task at this point will have a refreshing effect.

After a lengthy spell of work on a song, try some quick, light-hearted aural tests. Play a dozen bars of music and ask the children how many beats there were in a bar. Ask them this *after* you have played the music. Done consistently, this ploy encourages them to listen carefully to whatever you play, not knowing what task you will set them. Or tell them that you are going to play a piece of music to them. Make it clear that it is not one that they already know. Then ask them to sing the note which they think should come next whenever you stop. Your halts should come immediately before each cadence point and the melody should of course be contrived as unambiguously as possible:

One of the attractive features of this 'missing note' game is the way in which the children respond when they find that they can do what you ask. To many of them music is a mysterious, almost magical, business, and to discover that they themselves are able to join in its creation delights them. The ability to extemporize fluently short, simple harmonized musical sentences on the piano is invaluable in this work. But a teacher who cannot do so is not therefore obliged to forfeit this useful device. He might 'compose' suitable material for the purpose beforehand, or use unharmonized tunes which can simply be sung or whistled.

Much of the music to be sung by the school choir should be prepared and learned in the ordinary class lessons. This not only saves time at the choir practice, but it gives those who are not in the choir the opportunity to become familiar with music which they will later hear performed by the rest. It also encourages the choir, when they come together, to be able to sing as a body something already partly prepared.

It has already been suggested that the atmosphere of the school choir-practice should differ from that of an ordinary lesson. Conversely, do not make the same demands in the singing class as you would at the choir practice. Perhaps the first aim in class-singing should be enjoyment. Achieve the best standards you can without harassing the children, but do not press for finer points of technique or spend too much time on exercises. You will soon learn to assess the optimum.

Never make children sing a song through a second time with a vague comment that it wasn't good enough. If you want them to repeat it in order to improve some feature, explain to them what you are looking for. A disgruntled approach on your part damps any enthusiasm they may have and will not foster it if it isn't already there.

Sometimes the teacher who complains that singing 'isn't good enough' does so because he does not really know himself precisely what is wrong with it. Learn to diagnose the reasons for poor results. Perhaps the singing is listless and the intonation flat because the class has been standing too long, or because you have kept them singing the same thing too often, or simply because the room has grown stuffy. If it is just that they are lazy and inattentive, remember that they are most likely to learn enthusiasm from your own attitude. Sharp singing is usually caused by forcing, and occasionally by over-anxiety. In the latter case, a change of activity is the best procedure.

Avoid stopping the class too often when they are singing. Major mistakes should be dealt with at once, but as a general rule it is better to let the children get the feel of a song by singing it through, while remembering yourself where the mistakes occurred. These can be dealt with separately afterwards. Sing back to the children their version of each mistake and see if they can tell you what is wrong. Their criticism is even more likely to produce an effective result than your own. Take advantage of this fact by dividing your singers into two or more groups and let one group sing while the others criticize them. Then get the critics to try to show the others how it should be done. Children take this seriously, and will do their utmost to correct errors pointed out in this way by their fellows.

It is a good idea to accustom the individual child to sing alone. Some children who have never done so before are very shy about singing in front of the rest of the class. This is particularly true of boys in mixed classes. Bear this in mind, and when you first ask children to sing by themselves, select only a few in turn and make sure that you ask only those who seem anxious to try, who can sing reasonably well, and are not timid. It is impossible to force a child to sing properly against his will, and it is foolish to try. Let these few children sing parts of the songs that the class is learning. Attempt to carry the thing off with a minimum of fuss—'See if you can sing this bit, Smith.' Subsequently add to those whom you ask until in time it is no more unusual to ask an individual child to sing than to ask him to read alone in front of his classmates. Perhaps the best time to start this is when you are preparing carols. The children will all be familiar with some of these and the atmosphere is right on such an occasion.

When children are no longer afraid of the sound of their own voices heard individually, the confidence, attack and tone in their combined singing is greatly enhanced. Encourage this confidence further by the way in which you accompany their singing. When children are learning a song the piano should naturally give them as much help as possible. The melody should be incorporated into the accompaniment and played with the utmost clarity and some emphasis. But once the song is reasonably familiar the melody should be omitted altogether. Indeed, it will encourage your singers to hold their part if you make a practice during rehearsal of cutting down the accompaniment to a minimum— perhaps leaving out whole bars at a time and just playing a rhythmic pattern with a chord here and there, or when there is a change of key.

At other times explain to them before they begin to sing that you are going to enjoy yourself at the piano this time. Tell them not to allow themselves to be put off by what you do. Then elaborate the accompaniment and see if they can still hold their part. Tricks of this kind not only help to give them increased confidence but also add touches of novelty to their musical experience and help to prevent the music lesson from becoming repetitious and the singers stale.

Attack is another quality to develop. When children are learning a song, their teachers too frequently start them by counting. If the song has an introduction, then that introduction should be learned as part of the song. See that the children are familiar with it and that they know at what point to add their voices.

Sometimes, more particularly in songs of the last fifty years, the introduction has what one might call a telescoped cadence— the first note of the song melody coinciding with the last note of the introduction:

('Time, you old gipsy-man'—Harold Greenhill. Novello)

The understanding teacher will sympathize with the latent musicianship of a child who, confronted with an example such as this, is so engaged in waiting for the introduction to come to an end that he fails to begin to sing before it does so. Yet often such engagingly musical behaviour is attacked by a teacher who has failed to note this feature of the music himself, and so has not seen the reason for his singers failing to make their entry.

A song introduction of this kind needs a short comment from the teacher. He should play it over to the class, suggesting that it sounds as if it is going to last longer than it in fact does. Then show them how the first note of the song comes in, not as they might expect, when the introduction is over, but at the very moment that its last note is reached. The teacher is then confiding in his class instead of drilling them. He will find, particularly where music-making is concerned, that this is a good policy.

If a song has no introduction at all—and some editions of folksongs and traditional ditties are in this class—always provide one. A bar or two of extemporization based on the melody is enough. But always play the same introduction so that your singers know just when to start. It is often a good idea to use the last bar or two of the song itself.

Make sure that you play the introduction at the same speed as you intend the class to sing, and always make your accompaniments very rhythmic. Playing with loose, wavering rhythm and frequent *rubato* produces sloppy, lifeless singing. After a *rallentando* resume the normal pace deliberately, and emphasize the pulse for a few beats. Breathe yourself when the singers have to breathe. This will help you to suggest in your playing the treatment and phrasing you expect from them.

If you have to interrupt the singing of a song, perhaps to go over some point of detail, and need to pick up again in the middle, make sure that you explain clearly just where you want the class to begin, and also where you yourself propose to start playing. This will usually be a few beats before the singers enter. Or if you mean to start them by counting, be sure to count aloud those beats which precede the singer's entry.

For instance, if the voices enter on the fourth beat of a bar of common time, then you should count the first three beats:

It is a mistake to use a stereotyped 'One, two,' whatever the
time of the piece, as this provides no guide as to the flow and
pulse of what follows:

Count aloud: 4 | 1 ♩ ♩ ♩ | ♩.
                   And did those feet.....

Count aloud: 3 4 | ♩ ♩♩ | ♩.
                     Bring me my bow.......

Count aloud: 1 and 2 ♪ | ♩ ♪♩ ♪ | ♩ ♪ |
                       There was a jol-ly mil-ler....

TWO-PART SINGING

Two-part songs make an interesting addition to the singing
lesson. Simple ones, rounds, and songs with descants can be
introduced in the upper classes of the junior school. Perhaps the
best introduction to two-part singing, which needs confidence,
experience and discipline, is made by dividing the class for
straightforward two-part exercises. The descending scale makes
good material for this:

Let each half of the class try out its own part separately to begin
with. You will see that in this example each part consists of a
simple descending scale with a slight adjustment at the close.
Second trebles, who begin first, sing down the whole octave and
then add two further notes: C sharp and D. First trebles, who
start two beats later, sing straight down to the keynote.

When each group is sure of its part, let them try singing in
combination. Children who have never done this sort of thing
before respond immediately to the effect of increased sonority
which even this simple exercise produces. They are at once
anxious for more. Let them sing it again with different vowel-

M.I.C.—3

sounds and in a variety of keys. Then while they are still enjoying this sense of achievement, launch them into learning a simple two-part song or a round.

To save keeping half the class idle while the rest learn a separate part, it is best to let the whole class learn both parts, dividing them afterwards. This means, too, that you can obtain greater variety—and incidentally more practice—by changing the parts round.

Remember that, although in a true two-part song both parts may be equal in strength, in a song with descant the melody itself should always be prominent. Always use a smaller group to sing a descant.

For the more demanding two- or three-part songs, don't be afraid to call special short rehearsals for each part in turn during lunch hours. Children who have never been asked to do this sort of thing voluntarily may be taken aback at first, but you can encourage them to see the value of such extra practice. And, especially if your rehearsal is slick and businesslike, with no time wasted, they will find the result worth while. So will you.

4. Teaching Notation

Teaching children to read and use notation is a demanding and a rewarding task. It can provide stimulating mental exercise for the child. But that is not its main purpose; and the teacher must always remember that he is teaching music and not arithmetic.

Those rather displeasing exercises in which barlines have to be inserted, or notes have to be grouped according to a given time signature, are all very well for promising instrumentalists to grapple with. For the average child in school they can spell misery. The teacher should ask himself from time to time *why* he is teaching notation. The answer should always be, 'To help the children make music.' Too often this branch of music is in danger of being taught in schools as an end in itself. In that case it becomes sterile, and can make some children hate the music lesson.

The introduction of simple instrumental music in schools in recent years has made possible an approach to the teaching of notation which reduces the danger of separating theory from practice. When every child in a class has a musical instrument at his disposal—whether it be a glockenspiel, chime bar, or just a wood block—his ability to join with others in musical performance provides both a reason and an incentive for him to learn to read music. And what he learns through practice will be more meaningful and memorable to him than an assortment of memorized facts.

Moreover, it is less than satisfactory if a child, after a considerable struggle, has learned that the names of the first three spaces in the treble stave are F, A, and C—but still has no idea of the sounds involved. With a glockenspiel in front of him, symbol and sound can be learned in association from the outset. It will not be necessary to explain here how much more easily the sounds of individual notes can be produced from an instrument than by singing them.

However, even the most lavish supply of classroom instruments will not automatically ensure that children *recall* differences of pitch. To learn to do so they must be given frequent opportunities to produce notes, not only on instruments but with their voices. A child can give a faultless performance of the notes F, A, and C on his glockenspiel; but, unless the teacher trains him to do so, he can remain quite unable to *sing* A and C after he has played F.

Thus, merely to link the teaching of notation with the development of instrumental work in schools will not provide an infallible path to success. For that reason, as well as because many schools have not yet acquired sets of classroom instruments, the two topics are considered in separate chapters here. It remains for the teacher to associate the work in learning to read with that in learning to sing and play, according to the resources available in his school. Success in this branch of music-teaching comes through developing singing, playing, and reading, side by side.

In what follows, then, there are some pointers to the way in which various aspects of notation can best be explained to children. The subject is complicated; and because most young music teachers are instrumentalists themselves (and accustomed to the use of notation), many of them underestimate the difficulty of introducing its use to children.

Remember that notation is designed to provide two principal kinds of information to the reader. It tells not only how a melody rises and falls, but also how long each sound lasts. These two functions become telescoped for the experienced musician, who can see at a glance the whole message that each note conveys. This is not so for the child, and it is best to introduce those two aspects of notation—pitch and rhythm—separately.

RHYTHM

Deal first with rhythm. It is the musical quality which you can expect to find quite strongly developed in almost every child. Sensitivity to pitch variation is not nearly so general among children, and the problem of pitch is better left for a time until they have learned to deal with very simple rhythmic notation, and have gained in confidence through their success in that field.

It is tempting to begin by showing them on the board semi-breve, minim, crotchet and quaver, and making them learn the value of each note. To do so enables you to set them problems to test their knowledge of these note values. This is almost the worst way to set about the task.

Let the children first meet notes as sounds, not symbols. Begin by tapping out a series of regular unaccented beats. Then show on the board how musicians write these sounds:

♩ ♩ ♩ ♩ ♩ ♩ ♩

Then get the class to 'perform' what you have written. Make sure that they clap only as many notes as appear on the board. That is the first fact for them to learn about standard notation—that the performer plays what the composer writes down.

Next, tap the same pattern again, but breaking an occasional beat into halves:

♩ ♩ ♫♩ ♩ ♩ ♫♩

Ask the children to describe what has happened. If you are patient and helpful you will get the answer you want. Then you can introduce them to the symbol for half-beat notes on the board. Don't start talking about crotchets and quavers—'whole notes' and 'half notes' are much more satisfactory in the early stages.

Before going any further, drill them frequently in the use of these two notes until every child has mastered their function. Tap out rhythmic phrases based on crotchets and quavers and get individual children to come out and try to write down on the board, a few notes each, what they hear:

1. ♩ ♩ ♫♩
2. ♩ ♫♩ ♩
3. ♩ ♫♫♩

Tap each phrase several times while they examine it and try to decide on its make-up. When you have several such patterns on the board, tap one and ask the children to identify it. And let them try to tap them too. A whole class given an unrestricted opportunity of tapping on desk-tops can produce an appalling amount of noise and quickly get out of control. Let them perform by tapping a finger on the open palm of the other hand. This produces a clear sound but is unlikely to stimulate a riot. Or ask individual children to tap the phrases separately.

At this stage some teachers will find the French Rhythm-Names useful. The children learn to pronounce these rhythmically so that the name itself reproduces the rhythm of the notes in question. It is as if the nonsense syllables that we often use in wordless singing ourselves had been codified. Thus, 'Pom-tiddy pom-pom' is easily recognizable as ♩ ♫♩ ♩. The French system is based on a similar practice which appears to have been adopted across the Channel by sergeant-drummers centuries ago to teach recruits to memorize drum-parts in army bands. Here are some examples:

A chart showing the French Rhythm-Names appears in Appendix IV on page 113.

Another more modern device which will be helpful at this stage, to both primary and secondary schools, has been evolved from the system introduced in Germany by Carl Orff. Like the French method, this one employs verbal rhythms to reproduce and pattern musical sounds; but here the words used come from everyday use. The teacher selects suitable examples to illustrate individual patterns, encouraging the children to suggest further examples. Popular makes of car, for instance:

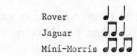

Or football teams:

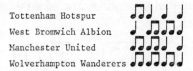

Tottenham Hotspur
West Bromwich Albion
Manchester United
Wolverhampton Wanderers

At this early stage you will also need to introduce the bar line.
Return to the series of unaccented beats tapped out on the desk:

 *etc.*

Then introduce a regular accent:

Ask the class what has happened. Make sure that you ask several
children this question. Don't stop asking if the first one happens
to give you the correct answer. There is sure to be a child here
and there who will think that the accented note is a *longer* note.
You must clear up this doubt before going any further.

When it is clear to the class that the accent is regular, you can
show them how we use bar lines to indicate the fact. Point out
that we *could* show the louder notes in red, or put a mark over
them. But it *happens to be the practice* to put a line in front of each
accented note. This divides the music up into regular groups,
called bars, and each bar begins with an accent. Test this by
tapping different pulses and by playing short melodies on the
piano for them to identify the time pattern.

If you made use of the names of football teams, for instance,
at an earlier stage, use them again at this stage to show how the
accents in the words correspond to the position of barlines in a
musical setting:

West Bromwich Albion

Wolverhampton Wanderers

With the addition of bar lines you can now contrive whole phrases based on the simple notes available. Give the older children opportunities of writing down for themselves what you tap:

$$2 \, \text{♩♩} \mid \text{♫♩} \mid \text{♫♩} \mid \text{♩♩} \, \|$$

The number of beats in a bar should now be shown as a plain figure at the beginning of the phrase.

By this time the minim can be introduced. Care is needed in this because a two-beat note cannot be adequately tapped or clapped. Use a chime bar or sing your first examples to make the extra length of the minim perfectly clear:

$$2 \, \text{♩♫} \mid \text{𝅗𝅥} \quad \mid \text{♫♫} \mid \text{𝅗𝅥}$$

When the children clap a rhythm containing a minim, they should represent its second beat by pressing the hands together:

♩ ♩ | 𝅗𝅥   Equals   tap, tap, | tap—press.

The length of time to be spent reaching this stage depends on the age of the children concerned. But, bearing in mind that the teaching of notation will occupy only a part of each music lesson, several weeks will be needed for young children to master the work described so far, and to apply it practically. Older children will cover the ground much more quickly. Frequent opportunities should be sought during their singing to refer to things which the children are learning about notation. Where some instrumental work is admitted to the classroom the points can be dealt with even more readily. Above all, avoid a tendency to separate theory and practice in your own mind.

PITCH

The first approach to the use of pitch notation is most easily made in conjunction with the use of pitch-playing percussion instruments. The topic will be taken up again in a later chapter dealing

with that activity. The present chapter, however, outlines aspects
of the subject which instrumentally trained pupils must not be
allowed to ignore.

Before proceeding to teach the notation of pitch, an intermediate
stage is advisable, particularly in the junior school. This new step
will introduce children to the 'block diagram' method of depicting
the rise and fall of melodies (already described in Chapter Two).
At this stage, rhythm and pitch should each be dealt with
separately.

Taking a simple and familiar phrase, the opening of 'Bobby
Shaftoe' for instance, the teacher first plays or sings the tune and
sets down the rhythm in the usual way:

2 ♫♫ | ♫♫ |

The children are then asked to listen to each note of the tune in
turn and to decide simply whether it goes up or down, or stays
in the same place. Strangely enough, it is when a note stays at
the same pitch as its predecessor that some children are confused.

As the children correctly decide whether each note in turn has
risen or fallen, the teacher should indicate its position pictorially
on the board:

There should as yet be no attempt to decide *how far* the notes rise
or fall, except perhaps to distinguish between large intervals and
very small ones. The information contained in the two diagrams
on the board may then be combined in a third diagram—which
will show the outline of the tune in standard notes, but excluding
the stave:

2 ♫♪ | ♪♫ |

Many short phrases of well-known melodies and songs that are
being learned can be dealt with in this way.

When the teacher feels confident that the children are conversant with the detail of this exercise, and when they are able to decide unhesitatingly whether rise or fall is involved between individual notes, then a start may be made on the third stage—the precise notation of pitch.

Here, once again, the teacher must not allow his own training and experience as a performer to blind him to the difficulties involved. Nor should he think that the methods employed to train an instrumentalist are necessarily the best to adopt in teaching notation to a classroom of children. Few pianists, for instance, are instinctively drawn to Tonic Sol-fa. But the system is a most useful aid in pitching intervals, and also in mastering the early stages of pitch-notation. Teachers, especially in the junior and infant school, should certainly make use of it. They must therefore be prepared to master its use themselves.

The danger with Tonic Sol-fa is that it is sometimes allowed to become an end in itself. Remembering that the standard notation is the staff, and that any future member of choral society or orchestra in your class will need to read the music provided, your aim should be to teach them to read staff notation. Tonic Sol-fa will help you to do so, both in the early stages and when you are dealing with the problems of calculating intervals.

Exercise the class *regularly* in singing short, simple tunes pointed out on and between the fingers of your own raised hand. Give them the pitch of *doh*, and then leave them to translate your gestures into sounds.

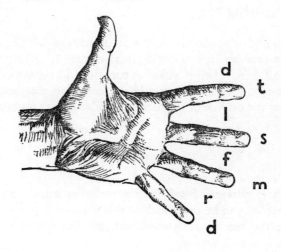

Make the exercises short, and aim for prompt reaction from the singers:

$$\text{d r m} - \text{|} \quad \text{f m r} - \text{|} \quad \text{m f s f} \text{|} \quad \text{m r d} - \text{||}$$

A few minutes devoted to this work in every music lesson will quickly develop children's sense of pitch, and at the same time will prepare them for an understanding of the layout of the stave.

At first they should sing as you point out each note of a tune, sometimes using sol-fa names, sometimes singing to a vowel. Then the process can be reversed: you sing, and they point out the notes on their own raised hands. They are then, in principle, taking down a melody at your dictation; and it is possible to check their accuracy by looking around as they do so. Stop from time to time in the course of a melody, to check that every child is pointing to the right 'note' on his hand.

Limit melodies at first to the range *d-s*, and ensure competence in step-wise tunes in that range before embarking on intervals. Some classes may need to gain familiarity with the sol-fa syllables by *naming* them as you point them out, before they are ready to sing them. In the early stages *doh* should be placed, as in the illustration above, on the little finger. You then have the whole range of an octave at your disposal without recourse to leger lines.

As far as possible, treat this exercise as a musical game, introducing it as a device to make a change of atmosphere in the course of a lesson. Two or three minutes spent in this way in every lesson will quickly produce results. Set out to develop an alert reaction from your class, and make sure that the exercises employed are always tuneful. Never point out disconnected notes for this work—even the simplest exercises should make musical 'sense'.

Children who have acquired skill at this preliminary exercise will be able to turn to work on the stave without trouble. Many teachers have found that first attempts to introduce the use of the stave otherwise come to grief, because some children cannot avoid thinking that the notes stand on the lines, and not in the spaces as well. A child who can sing 'from the hand' is less likely to fall into this trap. Even when the children are able to read from the stave, they should continue to sing from the hand as well. The ability to sing at sight is something developed through regular practice; and this device enables that practice to be obtained with a minimum of fuss, at a moment's notice, in the course of every lesson if need be.

The first lesson on the stave should follow naturally from this work by introducing to the children the five lines of the stave as a mere extension of the fingers of the teacher's hand, held against the blackboard. It is most important not to clutter up early lessons in notation—especially those with young children—with matter that is not essential. The clef, key signatures, and other incidental things must come later. They will only confuse at this stage. Omit them.

When singing from the hand, the children have grown accustomed to find *doh* on the little finger. For their first work with the written stave, the bottom line should represent *doh* in the same way. Don't allow yourself to fret if placing it there seems to call for a key signature. It has been remarked elsewhere that an important part of the psychological equipment of a teacher is the ability to decide what to omit as well as what to include in a lesson. The good teacher is wise in skilful omissions. This is a case in point. Pacify yourself by remembering that the notes on a stave depend on the choice of clef; and at the moment you are not using one at all.

CLEFS

No reference has yet been made to the alphabetical names of the notes, and for that reason the Treble Clef has not been included in the work so far outlined. But during the course of early lessons in the notation of pitch, the teacher should introduce the manner of naming the notes. If your course includes instrumental work, the point will have arisen there; if not, a start should be made at this stage. Make sure that the children see how the notes are named successively through the lines and spaces:

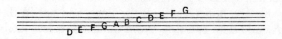

You will have to show them why we do not go right on through the alphabet—that G is followed, not by H, but by returning to A. This is perhaps best done by playing an octave of the major scale on the piano and drawing their attention to the relationship between the first note and its octave. If you tell them that a man and a boy who attempt to sing the same note will produce sounds which are related in this way, it will help them to see your point. Let them listen to a note and its octave played simultaneously. Point out the way in which the two notes blend as if they were one. Then demonstrate for them the clash that results when you sound a seventh or ninth. Let them experience the feeling of *arrival* as the notes of the scale ascend and the octave is reached.

The time-honoured mnemonics for the names of the lines and spaces may certainly be used. But if you believe in teaching Why as well as What, you will explain the layout of the stave as a whole first.

Once the names of the notes are known the function of the Treble Clef should be explained. Show the children how it started its life as a letter G and that it is there to fix the position of that note:

A class which has reached this stage of work in notation is ready to increase its skill in sight-singing by working from one of the published collections of graded material. Some suitable books are included in the lists at the end of this book. There is always the temptation for a teacher who is developing instrumental music with his classes to feel that sight-singing exercise is not necessary. This is a mistake. Instrumental players are certainly developing familiarity with the use of notes; but they are not necessarily acquiring the ability to *hear* the notes before they play them. Sight-singing should not be neglected in classes which have the additional opportunities for music-making that instrumental work affords.

Music-teaching is complicated by a situation which does not arise in the teaching of other subjects. Certain children in a class will perhaps be learning to play an instrument by private tuition. They will already know many of the things that you are so slowly explaining to the rest. They will be impatient with your slow progress and will be anxious to display their superior knowledge to the rest of the class. It is dangerously easy for the young teacher to be misled by a few children of this sort into believing that the whole class is learning the things that these few know.

Make sure that you find out which children in any class have private music lessons. Find an opportunity of taking them on one side and confiding to them that you realize they will already know quite a number of the things that you are going to teach the rest. Explain to them that they will have to be patient. But make it clear that they should follow all that you say because some of the things will be new to them. Flatter them a little without making them too self-important, and then make sure that you let someone else answer the more elementary questions that you put to the class.

Quite often, as it happens, you will find that it is not always the child who has had the benefit of private music lessons who is the most successful. He may be learning to play an instrument, but his ear-training is often surprisingly neglected. Over-confidence enters into it too.

DOTTED NOTES

As work in rhythm proceeds, the question of dotted notes will arise. These are best introduced when dealing with melodies of three beats in a bar, a dotted minim making up the last bar. Children who are first introduced to the dotted note as a dotted crotchet can easily become obsessed with the idea that a dot adds *half a beat* to a note's value. This understandable mistake is avoided if the dotted minim is introduced first. They can then see that the value of the dot depends on the value of the note to which it is added.

Dotted rhythms cause many children a great deal of bother. They find it very difficult to distinguish between

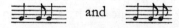

The teacher should be very patient when this confusion arises and should give them many opportunities of meeting this rhythmic figure and becoming familiar with it. French Rhythm-Names can help here.

If the children are shown how to beat time themselves, using the conventional gestures, they can test such rhythms for themselves.

The teacher can help them by showing how a dotted crotchet lasts longer than one of a conductor's beats—that it goes on sounding 'after he has turned the corner'.

The notation itself is best introduced by following three distinct stages. First, considering the *sounds* represented by these notes: 3 ♩ ♫♩. Then noting the effect *in sound* of an added tie: 3 ♩‿♫♩. Finally, transcribing the same note pattern without the use of the tie: 3 ♩. ♪♩.

Never make the mistake of giving exercises which are too complicated. It takes a long time for the whole class to be competent in dealing with the problems involved in this work. The over-zealous teacher will only make the less-capable child despondent. Teaching which is geared to the standard reached by the bright members of any class produces an ever-increasing section of the less able who lose interest, lose hope, and finally give up altogether.

RESTS

Rests should be explained quite early in the scheme of work. The children will meet them in their songs.

As far as school work is concerned, it is a great pity that the continental form of the crotchet rest is not universally used. The children can get to know this as a 'tea-leaf' ≩ and learn that it is worth one beat. But as the English version is also found in some editions, one of the first points to clarify is the distinction between ≣ worth one beat, and ≢ worth a half beat. I have found it a help to some pupils to provide a mnemonic in which the resemblance between the shape of their two rests and the first letters of their note-names is employed: ϟ *rotchet* and ϟ *uaver*.

This distinction, like that between ≣ worth two beats and ≣ worth four beats, is something that just has to be learned. You can perhaps help the children by explaining that the four-beat rest *sinks* below the line because it is larger, while the two-beat rest *floats* because it is smaller. But these facts are best learned, like other routine matters, by frequent reference to them. Expression marks, on the other hand, should be dealt with as they occur in the songs and pieces which the children learn.

TIME SIGNATURES

Time signatures in children's early exercises should be limited to single figures. The significance of the lower figure in a time signature is probably best dealt with in connection with songs which the class is learning.

Show that a conductor can beat three-in-a-bar time in several different ways. He can beat very slowly, very fast, or at quite a moderate pace. Yet in each case the music still has the same number of beats in each bar. Play three different examples on the piano to emphasize this and to give the class full opportunity of agreeing with your contention. Then explain that although the number of beats in a bar in each piece is the same, it is the *kind* of beat which is different. Some of the beats take much longer than others. In other words, when the conductor's beats are longer, this is because the notes in the music are long notes. Show them some examples of this:

In each case the conductor will beat three times in a bar, but his arm will move much quicker for the bottom example than for the top one.

When you have carried the class with you so far, explain that the top number in a time signature tells you how many beats the conductor will make in a bar. The bottom number tells you what sort of beat it will be.

If each of the conductor's beats is

worth	𝅝	then the bottom number is 1
,,	𝅗𝅥	,, ,, ,, ,, ,, 2
,,	𝅘𝅥	,, ,, ,, ,, ,, 4
,,	𝅘𝅥𝅮	,, ,, ,, ,, ,, 8

The children will easily be able to see why these particular numbers are used. Help to bring the point home by putting up on the board a few simple examples of bars of different value, and get the class to calculate a time signature for each. Do this orally so that the whole class can follow each part of the process:

See that the answer is arrived at in controlled stages—first working out the top number, and then deciding on the bottom one.

Frequent reference to the matter of time signatures as they occur on copies of songs which the children are learning, and the inclusion of them in their future dictation exercises, will be advisable before you can expect every child to become conversant with all this.

Do not attempt to deal with compound time signatures except with secondary school children in the second or third year. Even here it is advisable to prepare the way by introducing them first aurally to a musical example such as Bach's 'Jesu, joy of man's desiring', with its clear 9/8 grouping in the oboe *obbligato*. The fact that there is a firm underlying three-in-a-bar pulse in the vocal part makes this particular piece an invaluable aid to your explanation.

Before you attempt to explain time signatures to a class, prepare your material and your explanations very carefully. Then reconsider them from the child's point of view, and see what loopholes you can find. If there are any, you can be sure that a class that is really following your explanation will find them.

KEY SIGNATURES

In their third year of this work Junior school children may be introduced to key signatures. In secondary schools the matter can be dealt with by the second year.

The best way, I have found, is to play up the scale for one octave from C. Then explain that you are going to do this again, but starting on another note, and you want the class to notice what happens. Begin to play on G. Pause on each note as the scale rises until you come to F natural. An attentive class will express their distaste vigorously when you reach this note. Something is wrong.

Ask them what is the matter with this note. Persevere until they can tell you that it needs to be raised. Then play G so that they can tell you that this is raising it too far. Then introduce them to the sound of F sharp. Explain it as a note half-way between F and G. Tell them that a sharp is a note raised half a degree, and finally show them the symbol on the board.

You will need to explain that the sign for a sharp is put *in front* of the note which it affects. Most children, understandably, expect to put the sign after the note—it is called F sharp after all.

Repeat this experiment later with the scale of D, getting the class to tell you which notes sound wrong when only naturals are played, and what needs to be done to correct them.

Then explain to them that, if a tune has D as the 'home-note', every time these notes which 'sound wrong' in the scale crop up they will sound wrong in the tune. And that to remedy this, an instruction is given at the beginning of the music to alter these notes whenever they occur. Children see the point if they are told that the sharps in the key signature provide what amounts to 'a season ticket'. Then show the orderly manner in which the sharps are inserted at the beginning of the stave:

and explain that although only one F carries a sharp, *all* the F's are affected by it; the same with C.

During the course of two or three successive lessons, investigate the scales of G, D and A in this way. Then introduce flats similarly. Start with the scale of F and let the children decide for themselves which notes 'sound wrong', and that, this time, these notes need to be lowered to produce the expected sound.

It is not necessary to explain and demonstrate this in keys with more than three sharps and flats. Once the principle is made clear, more complicated examples can be dealt with as they arise. But make sure that the sharps and flats used by the children in their own work are written down clearly, and that their position is shown as accurately on the stave as that of notes.

In all this work the children must learn to write carefully and clearly. Explain to them that tiny inaccuracies in the use of notation will produce wrong sounds in performance. Children must be shown how to form note-shapes tidily—many of them substitute a small letter *d* for a minim if this is not corrected. Most attempts at a treble clef produce the outline of a knotted bootlace if the teacher is not firm about clarity.

As soon as a class begins to write musical dictation it is advisable to show them the time-saving version of a crotchet, using instead of the normal round-headed note (which takes so long to draw) one whose head consists of a single stroke of pen or pencil:

As long as careful distinction is made as to the exact position of the note, this symbol is adequate. It is a good idea to make the stroke horizontal when the note lies in a space, and diagonal when it rests on a line. This reduces the chance of confusion in reading the work afterwards:

Minims and semibreves should be built up from two short curves, rather than drawn as ovals:

The treble clef itself should also be copied from the board several times, and built up in stages so that the youngest children learn its design properly:

EXAMINATIONS AND TESTS

It has already been stressed that music must gain a normal place in the school curriculum and not be allowed to assume an unusual character. It is desirable therefore to include music in the subjects which make up the sessional examinations. Simple rhythmic and melodic dictation, the recognition of short extracts from known songs written in staff notation, questions dealing with time, and key, and general musical knowledge should be included. While not wishing to make the examination an end in itself, the teacher will see that the advantages of holding examinations in other subjects apply equally to music. In secondary schools where music is healthy, the subject can take its place with the rest in both G.C.E. and C.S.E. examinations.

5. *Teaching Singing*

Not every teacher is gifted with a good singing voice. But it is essential that he should use what voice he has to the best advantage. He must be able to 'pattern' examples to the children and use his own voice so confidently and easily that the children will do the same.

The enthusiast will therefore be anxious to secure some good vocal training himself before he guides others. A course of private singing lessons will give a considerable boost to a teacher's skill in this direction, as well as increasing his confidence in his own ability.

If it were possible to learn the secrets of voice-production from a book, the preceding paragraph would not have been necessary. What follow are merely a few suggestions, practical tips on class singing and choir training. But the reader must realize that, before these work successfully, he must learn to assess the results of his work by acquiring an acute critical sense where children's voices are concerned. He must find opportunities of listening to well-trained children's voices—in other schools, at school choir festivals, at churches with a reputation for good choral standards, from recordings and radio performances.

The suggestions made here are not magic formulae, and their use will not *per se* achieve the desired results. The teacher must use his own ears and compare the sounds that his children produce with those made by other more expert choirs.

BREATHING

Good singing depends largely on efficient breathing. Ask a child to take a deep breath and he will usually brace back his knees, push forward his pelvis, clench his teeth, throw up his shoulders, push out his chest, take an exaggerated sniff through his nose, and hold it with a look of earnest martyrdom in his glazing eyes. This used to be the method favoured in the gymnasium in my own schooldays, and though I am assured that it is no longer fashionable, children still do it.

Everything is wrong with this as far as breathing for singing is concerned. The first essential is relaxation. The singer must stand loosely. Muscular tension as displayed in clenched fists, braced knees and frowning faces, is fatal to good tone production. Let your children stand with feet slightly apart, and then go through a pantomime of drooping with them—all muscles slack, the arms hanging lifeless at their sides, the head falling forward on the neck. After this, recover a comfortable pose. Then let them feel for the bottom edge of their front ribs and place the

hands lightly on each side. They should then breathe in *with a quick gasp through the open mouth*. Remind them how an expert swimmer opens his mouth for a quick breath as he passes through the water. That is what is wanted. The chest must not be allowed to move upwards and the shoulders must not rise. Instead the children should try to make the bottom ribs, on which their hands are placed as a guide, move outwards and towards their sides.

You cannot tell children exactly how to do this, any more than you can tell them how to waggle their ears. But let them watch you and try to copy what you do while you move around demonstrating what you want, and checking their efforts. Bear in mind that unless you have already had some good vocal training, you will need to practise breathing in this way yourself. It is not easy, and requires different processes from those of ordinary breathing.

The expression 'a deep breath' is so frequently and loosely used that we usually miss its true significance. Yet it means just what it says: that the breath is taken right down to the base of the lungs, thus depressing the diaphragm. When this occurs, the lungs are accommodating much more breath than ordinarily. This is what forces the lower ribs outwards and sideways, and enables one to confirm the occurrence.

Let the class see the advantage of this new way of breathing by showing them how long a single properly taken breath can last. Choose a convenient note in your vocal compass and, after taking a deep breath inconspicuously, begin to sing, counting 1, 2, 3, 4, and onwards at a steady pace as long as your breath holds. You will probably reach a number in the thirties without any trouble and the children will be quite impressed.

Give them a chance to try this for themselves. Make them empty their lungs first by expelling the air in a quick rush (tell them to imagine that they are breathing on a mirror to polish it). Follow this at once by a deep breath of the kind already described, and then start them counting on a note already indicated. To be effective this exercise must be carried out by the whole class together.

The teacher should give his instructions clearly first, and then see that each action is carried out unanimously when he gives the word: 'Breathe OUT, IN,' 'Count 1, 2, 3,' etc. Unless it is controlled at each stage, an exercise of this kind can easily develop into a riot. And given the opportunity, the wittier ones are always ready to sneak little breaths on the way, and go on counting into the sixties.

BREATH CONTROL

This same exercise is also useful because it can be used to demonstrate breath-control. Many singers, especially children, waste their breath by expelling it too quickly as they sing. That is another reason why the 'chests out' type of breathing already described is so unsatisfactory. What felt like an enormous breath was taken and held under such tension that its release was bound to be too fast. Breathiness in singing, and the weak tone that characterizes it, are often due to this.

In good singing the breath is not allowed to escape. It is controlled so that only the necessary amount passes out at a time. Tell the children that they should sing as a teapot pours, and not as a hose-pipe forces water out in a jet. Some expert choir-trainers, in order to produce that pure restrained voice which is characteristic of our best cathedral choirs, have practised breath-control to an amazing degree. While practising, their choir-boys have had to hold a small mirror close to their mouths as they sang. If the mirror clouded then the boys knew that their breath-control was not good enough.

A superlatively restrained sound of the kind produced by cathedral choristers is not, in my view, wanted in class singing: perhaps even less in a school choir. But this is an illuminating example of the importance of breathing and breath-control in tone production. Faulty breathing is the cause of a great deal of poor singing. Most children, unless they are shown how to breathe properly, content themselves with miserable little sniffs taken at random in all the wrong places. Phrasing, tone and sonority all suffer on this account.

VOCAL REGISTERS

When children sing they are really employing two different voices—one for their top notes and another for the bottom ones. The dividing-line occurs at about the note A in the treble stave:

When they sing a melody that passes from one of these registers to the other, they have to make what amounts to a vocal gear-change. If the melody is moving downwards, from head-register to chest-register, this change is effected automatically. But when they sing a rising melody, it has to be negotiated carefully to be achieved.

Now many children, especially boys, do not always make this change. It is the same with some of us who drive motor-cars, and labour our engines when we should really have changed gear. If the chest voice is used for notes higher than its real range, rough harsh notes result. The listener feels that the singer is shouting.

In some schools, something akin to that questionable activity known as 'community singing' is the only form of music-making. And many boys, especially those anxious to assert their toughness, whose singing has been limited to this sort of thing, never use their head voices at all. As a result, they produce coarse, brassy sounds through their whole vocal range. Girls do it too, but usually to a less extent.

To wean them away from this, and to prevent it happening to others, children's singing exercises should always be framed so that the voice begins in the head register and descends. In this case, the change from one register to the other is automatic. It will be necessary to make sure that the child is using his head voice to start with. But if you get your class to sing softly at first, and make sure that they stand in a relaxed position, this is not likely to present much difficulty. Forcing of the chest voice up into the top register is invariably accompanied by a tense stance, frowning, and muscular restriction under the jaw.

Downward scales starting on upper D and sung lightly make excellent exercises. Encourage lightness and prevent forcing by singing them quickly and rhythmically. Repeat them, starting on successive semitones up to F, and use sounds such as La and Doh. Avoid hard vowels like Ah while there is a danger of shouting. Remember that a scale need not be a bald series of equal notes. A simple rhythmic pattern makes it more interesting as well as encouraging light easy singing of the kind you need.

Allegretto

Devise piano accompaniments to all scales and vocal exercises you mean to use, and learn to play them in all keys. The feeling of variety that a skilful piano accompaniment can give to vocal exercises is like jam round a pill. A decorated form of scale is a useful exercise to develop light agile singing.

Make sure that there is no sliding from one note to the next, and that the first note of each triplet gets clear accentuation.

TONE PRODUCTION

Once children have learned to enjoy singing the teacher can afford to begin the task of licking their vocal tone into shape. Good robust singing is best developed from good quiet singing. It is better to nourish good soft tone until it grows, than to try to trim down a roar. This will mean that the children have to abandon some of their more zestful vocal efforts for the time being. Consequently it is advisable for a new teacher to postpone this work until he has won the confidence of his pupils, and has given them first an unhampered opportunity of discovering—perhaps for the first time in their school experience—that singing can be a pleasant occupation.

To develop a good pure sound, the voice should be directed to the point where nose and forehead meet. Unfortunately, it is impossible to describe exactly how this is done. But it is possible for the singer to know when he has achieved it, because the vibration can be felt as a tickling sensation in the cavities immediately behind the top of the nose. The teacher is advised to try the instructions that follow for himself and to go through the various stages vocally.

To *encourage* vocal production of the kind desired the singer should hum gently on a convenient note (round about middle A) to the sound 'nn' (not 'mm'), keeping the lips and teeth slightly apart as he does so. Raise the eyebrows a little and open the nostrils as you hum, concentrating on the point behind the top of the nose. The tongue must lie flat and unbunched in the mouth, the tip just touching the lower teeth. A few trials will usually produce the sensation described, often coupled with an awareness that the sound of the note is clearer because it is being amplified by the nasal cavities.

This sound is the seed from which good vocal tone can be readily developed. Although it is soft, it is already more clear and telling than ordinary humming. But attempts to boost this sound too quickly will make it lose its quality. Having carefully produced this clear hummed note, if the singer then opens his mouth and utters a full-throated 'Ah' he will certainly obtain the volume he requires, but, almost inevitably, the purity of the sound will be destroyed.

To avoid this, the act of changing from humming to vocalizing should be gradual and controlled. The hummed note should be very carefully transformed into a sung note by the addition of the vowel sound 'ee'. Make this change very gently so that, although the vehicle for the sound is altered, its quality remains the same. Make sure that no change occurs in the position of mouth and throat—everything must remain completely relaxed. It is difficult to ruin the sound by this tiny adjustment, but it can be done. For instance, any attempt to increase the volume considerably at this stage will lead to muscular tension in the jaws and nostrils. This will immediately produce a fierce reedy sound which is useless.

Practise this change carefully several times, and listen critically yourself to the resulting sounds. When you are satisfied that you are obtaining the proper nasal resonance, follow up the change to 'ee' by a further careful widening of the mouth to produce the sound 'ay'. Make quite sure that the voice is still directed as before. Finally open to the sound 'oh'. Do not try to make a lot of sound, just let the voice come out by itself. By this gradual and controlled process the clear but soft hummed note gains sufficient resonance to be useful and does not need to be pushed from the mouth.

Once the teacher has learned for himself to control and direct his voice in this way, he can introduce children to the process.

Take each stage very slowly at first, making quite sure that the children understand what is wanted of them, and checking first of all that the hummed sound which is the foundation of the whole process is properly produced. Move around among the singers as they work, checking for muscular tension as shown in frowning faces and projecting jaws. As you stand behind a child, feel under his jaw with your finger-tips to see if there is any constriction or rigidity. If there is, let him feel for himself. Then make him swallow, to relax the muscles, and try again. Above all, listen to the sounds that each child produces. It is not necessary to make them sing alone if you move among them while they sing together.

It is unwise to use the same vowel sound for all vocal exercises. 'Ah' is a dangerous vowel because it encourages hardness. Reserve it for an occasional strengthening exercise once good tone has been produced, but never make it a standard for vocalizing. Some church choir-boys appear to exercise exclusively to 'oo'. As a result they produce the horrible 'choristers' hoot' which distorts all vowels to a meaningless approximation. Choristers who sing 'Hooly Ghoost' and a carol which begins 'Soolent Noot' do so because they have unwittingly come to regard 'oo' as the normal vehicle for singing and all their production is coloured by it.

Change the vowels used in exercises so that there is no danger of such habitual distortion. Use 'oo' and 'ah' far less frequently than such sounds as 'doh', 'lă', and 'may'. Remember that humming encourages good tone, and that all exercises need not be sung loudly.

THE ADOLESCENT VOICE

In encouraging the older boys in a secondary school to use their 'baritone' voices, the teacher will be careful to avoid allowing them to strain for notes beyond their reach. It is advisable to find what each boy's potentialities are before launching on to anything at all demanding.

This can be done without making each boy sing alone—a thing which, at any rate to begin with, most boys of this age will be unwilling to do. Remember that you will probably have to coax them to sing at all. Play the note A (at the top of the bass stave) and ask all your singers to sing down the scale together, counting aloud on each note as they descend. Tell them to stop individually when they find it at all difficult to go any lower, and urge them not to try to reach for notes which do not come easily. When they have done so, collect from each boy the last number he sang and record it against his name.

Then start again on D (third line up in the bass stave) and repeat the process singing upwards. In this case it is even more necessary to emphasize to them the risk of straining for notes which they cannot reach comfortably. A return of numbers will now give you the upper notes of each boy's compass, and you will be able to visualize your singers as first or second baritones—perhaps as potential tenors and basses. You should find that between them they can cover a range of about an octave, from one C to the other, and with luck a little more. Individual boys may exceed this by several notes.

The best teachers for boys of this age are of course men who have learned to sing properly themselves. But there is one useful tip to pass on to them which will help them to produce their notes in the right way, and which makes strain and misuse of the voice far less likely. Demonstrate to them how, since they lost their treble voices, an 'Adam's apple' has formed in the throat, and show them how this rises and falls as they speak.

Then point out to them that in good singing the Adam's apple is *not allowed* to rise in the throat. Put the tip of your finger on your own Adam's apple (if you are a man) and sing up the scale in that uncontrolled manner which allows it to rise. Then repeat the scale, tucking your chin back a little, and show them how, merely by 'willing' it to do so, it can be kept at the same level in the throat, with an immediate improvement in the tone of the voice. Then let them try this for themselves—all singing up the scale gently together, with a finger-tip touching the Adam's apple to test their success. Remember to check for this control in all their singing. Harsh, forced singing at this age is not only ugly, it is also downright harmful to the forming voice.

Apart from unison songs of the simpler type which can be found easily—but which may need transposing—there are also several collections of pieces for school choirs in the combination Soprano, Alto, Bass. Many of these make useful material to begin on because the music is contrived so that the tune itself is in the bass, not in the treble. This is an important consideration for boys who have had no previous experience in holding a part, or of reading in the bass clef.

Although girls' voices do not undergo the same drastic changes as boys' at this age, yet there is frequently an unsettled condition in many girls' vocal organs between the ages of twelve to fifteen or so. Many of them suffer from huskiness, their compass often changes—high voices become lower, and vice versa. Usually these things are purely temporary, and the teacher must be careful not to try to develop into a mature contralto a girl of thirteen or fourteen who has suddenly found some extra notes at the bottom of her normal range. The policy with girls should be the same as with boys of this age—do not treat their voices as if they were the voices of adults. Treat them with extreme care, avoid trying to develop powerful notes at the extremes of their compass, and do not urge them to things which they cannot do easily.

DICTION

A great deal of the choir-trainer's task is concerned with *words* as well as with music. A very marked improvement in most class singing can be achieved quite quickly by seeing that proper attention is given to the delivery of vowels and consonants. Exercise *Speech* as well as *Song*.

Let your singers say the five-vowel sounds 'ah-ee-ĕ-oh-oo', exaggerating the facial movements as they do so. Then let them sing the same five sounds to a single sustained note. Divide them into rival teams for mutual criticism. You will find, and they will not fail to notice too, that some children attempt to sing these five different sounds without perceptibly changing the shape of their mouths. A few pocket mirrors (to allow the most poker-faced to see themselves) can help here.

Tongue-twisters and similar tags make useful exercises both for speech and singing. Let the class *whisper* such things, stressing the consonants, and let them sing them at a brisk pace to simple tunes:

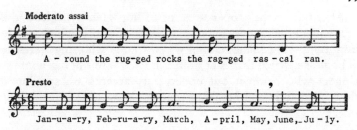

Moderato assai

A - round the rug-ged rocks the rag-ged ras - cal ran.

Presto

Jan-u-a-ry, Feb-ru-a-ry, March, A - pril, May, June, Ju - ly.

Explain that you want them to sing the *notes* softly, but the *words* loudly. It can be done—let them listen to the telling effect of that voiceless enunciation known as a stage-whisper. Show them that without using the vocal cords at all you can utter an instruction which can be clearly understood in a quiet room. Let them try it in turn—make it a game where conspiratorial whispers are necessary—and see if everyone can hear what each child tries to say.

Watch final consonants particularly. There are three very common faults connected with them:

(i) Their total omission: 'Nigh' an' day';
(ii) Attaching to a subsequent vowel: 'Nigh tanday';
(iii) Over-emphasis: 'Nighter ander day'.

Demonstration, explanation and exercise can cure all these faults—particularly with singers who have been helped to realize that an audience wants to hear the words of a song as well as its melody.

Even more care is required where *groups* of consonants occur: 'soFTLy', 'THRiFT', 'STReNGTH', 'maGNify', deSTRuction'. And if the same consonant ends one word and begins the next, specially thoughtful enunciation is needed to avoid distortion. Many listeners are left in doubt as to the final word in this couplet:

> Bright the vision that delighted
> Once the sight of *Judah's seer*.

Facial mobility, considerably exaggerated at first, will help to improve children's performance not only because it helps them to enunciate clearly but also because it makes them conscious of the importance of the words, and of the need to deliver them carefully.

Attention to the proper stressing of important syllables and the consequent deliberate under-emphasis of those which are less important will enhance choral work. Choirs who sing 'Jerusalem is built as a settee that is at unitee in itself' are singing nonsense; singers who hammer out unnecessary accents are spoiling the flow of melody and breaking spacious phrases into insignificant ones:

O rud-dier THAN the cher-ry, *etc.*

LINE AND PHRASING

In this latter case they are led to do so by the way in which the melody rises on 'than'. With untrained voices there is always a tendency to sing high notes louder than low ones. Most children's choirs attempting Parry's *England** produce a series of exaggerated thumps in the phrase:

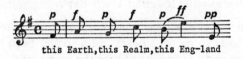

this Earth,this Realm,this Eng-land

(Apart from actually singing 'Thi Searth, thi Srealm, thi Seng-land'!) Accents are clearly called for here, but not the hammer-blows so often heard, which destroy the line of the phrase by breaking it up into two desperate acrobatic leaps and a hair-raising swoop.

The fault is even more pronounced in the first verse where the same melody carries the words

by *Nature, for* her *pur*pose,

and where a heavy accent on 'for' and the disjointed treatment already described produces a most unhappy effect.

To prevent this tendency to over-emphasis on high notes, when it occurs exercise on a series of rising sequences, explaining

---

* Year Press Book, No. 156. (A. & C. Black.)

to the children that you want them to avoid 'thumping' the high
note in each group:

Encourage them instead to sing the whole passage lightly,
emphasizing the first note and deliberately glossing over the
highest note in each group:

This is another case in which the teacher should sing both the
right and the wrong version to the class for their criticism.

Parry's *England* provides yet another example of the need for
subtlety in phrasing, and the absolute necessity of preparing
songs carefully before teaching them. Traps of this kind con
stantly occur in strophic songs and hymns, which employ the
same melody for a number of different verses. In the second
verse the melody itself suggests an appropriate breathing-point
in the line:

this bles-sed plot, ✳ this Earth,this Realm,this Eng-land

But in the first verse at the same point, an entirely different
treatment is called for. The children will tend automatically to
take a breath during the long note on the word 'built':

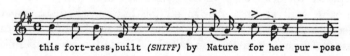

this fort-ress,built *(SNIFF)* by Nature for her pur-pose

The teacher must anticipate this, demonstrating how the sense
of the words is marred by an interruption at this point, and
inviting the class to suggest a more appropriate breathing place.

M.I.C.—5

Obviously the breath must be taken after 'fortress', the word 'built' being sung with a *crescendo* to carry the voices on warmly and with impetus to the end of the phrase:

this fort-ress, ❋ built by Nature for her pur‑pose

TEACHING A NEW SONG

Before teaching a song to a class, the teacher should always go through it carefully first, trying to discover points of this kind for himself before he confronts the class with the task of learning to sing it. He should edit his own copy, marking in breathing-points, phrasing, any difficult intervals or other snags, and noting the places where modifications in the accompaniment may be necessary to help the class while it is learning the song. He should practise the accompaniment so that he can play it without having to concentrate on that task alone. In the classroom he must be able to play it and look round the room, and perhaps talk, as he does so.

In looking through the song beforehand the teacher should try to conjure up in imagination the sound of his own singers performing it. It does not take very long to get to know a group of singers well enough to identify their principal idiosyncrasies, and most untrained children produce the same series of vocal shortcomings. With increasing experience the young teacher will find that he can put his finger on most of the points in a particular song where a class is likely to go astray—a faulty interval, lack of breath to sustain a final note, uncertain attack, rhythmic in-accuracy, loss of pitch, poor diction and all the rest. He is then prepared to deal with these points if they arise—and they probably will at first. Above all, he knows where to expect mistakes, and in the flurry of playing the song through with the class the first few times, he will be left with a more definite impression than that 'something went wrong'.

When introducing the new song to the class, bear in mind that it consists of both words and music, and give the children full opportunity of realizing the significance of both. Let them read through the words together to begin with, and help them to see the meaning of this difficult word, or that poetic allusion. Give them some idea of the background of the song, if there is something to be gained from that. There is no excuse for allowing a child to utter what appears to him as nonsense.

The method to adopt in presenting the music will, of course, vary according to the children's age and experience. But as soon as children have begun to learn about notation, the teacher will be anxious to make each new song an opportunity for gaining familiarity with the use of the printed note. With the youngest and least experienced, it will be enough for them to follow each note of the tune on their copies as it is played, and to notice how the notes rise and fall on the paper. Resist strongly any temptation to use a new song as sight-reading material. You can kill a song stone dead by doing this—no one will *want* to sing afterwards.

Let such young children, or those who have not yet acquired much skill in notation, listen to the tune first. Omit the introduction on this occasion, telling them you are going to start where the voice part begins, and play or sing through the first verse, emphasizing the melody. Then get them to follow the notes carefully in their copies while you play it again. It is advisable to stop sometimes to see that everyone is trying to keep with you in the vocal score. An occasional check of this kind makes for greater effort on the part of the lazier child, who may otherwise be quite prepared to sit idle—especially if you appear to be engrossed in the task of playing. Remember that you are still controlling a class as you play, and learn to look at them, not at the piano.

These two successive hearings of the music, together with the attention required to follow the outline of the melody on the copies, should give the class some idea of the tune. On the third playing get them to try to sing it with the piano—but ignoring the words altogether. See that they point to the notes as they sing them. Don't stop for small mistakes; aim at allowing the general trend of the whole passage to come home to the class. But notice where mistakes occur and deal with each in turn afterwards. If a difficult passage lies high in the compass, transpose it for repeated practice.

When the tune is reasonably secure, then add the words, drawing the children's attention first to any special difficulties—

such as syllables which are sung to more than one note, (*a*) and (*b*), or awkward intervals (*c*)—and practise these in isolation before singing the whole verse through:

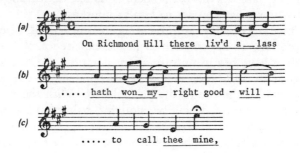

Make this an opportunity of explaining how the slurs in the music are used to indicate that the notes share a syllable.

Finally, draw their attention to the introduction. Let the class hear it several times, following in their copies, and then rehearse their entry by playing the introduction through again and telling them to sing just the first note of the song at the appropriate moment. Do this several times. Once they have managed to begin correctly, omit the accompaniment to their first note and see if they have the confidence to sing it firmly without the help of the piano.

The older children, as their familiarity with notation increases, will require much less help in reading the melody, and they should be encouraged to sing it from the copies—without the words of course—after hearing it played through once only. Help them, particularly in the tricky passages, by playing the melody firmly as they sing, but occasionally, in sections where the tune is straightforward, subdue the piano part and see how successfully they can negotiate short passages for themselves. As their confidence and ability increase this can happen more frequently.

It will be obvious that, quite apart from the educational advantage involved in acquiring such a new skill, increasing ability to read from the score means that children can meet a greater variety of music in the time available. The rather dreary business, from their point of view as well as your own, of teaching songs 'parrot-fashion', will become less and less necessary.

SCHOOL CHOIR FESTIVALS

Many teachers whose children take part in combined school choir festivals must find that to teach the number of songs required by rote in the time available monopolizes the whole of their class-work for many weeks of the year. Indeed, in some schools the approach of the festival is marked by considerable disorganization of the time-table. It may appear impressive when eventually scores of children perform these songs from memory, but knowing the hackwork involved and the amount of sheer drilling that has to go into the preparation of such performances I look forward to the day when these young singers are encouraged to work, even on the day of the concert if necessary, from copies of the music. Children can learn not to bury their noses in the copies and to look at the conductor quite as easily as they can learn the whole concert repertoire off by heart.

CHOOSING SONGS

In choosing songs for children there are three main considerations. Select things which they can enjoy, make sure that the difficulties involved are not too great or the vocal range too wide, and be certain that the music is good. Although you will be anxious to use music which pleases you, don't overlook the fact that it is the children who do the singing. They cannot give their best with a piece that requires adult perception or mature technique. (Avoid songs which contain many semitones.) But in your anxiety to find something which will please them, don't lower the musical standard. Old-fashioned ballads, Strauss waltzes with words tacked on, and sentimental songs are not to be recommended. Don't let your colleagues, or your headmaster, talk you into putting such things in a concert programme 'to please the audience'. Remember that you are not only teaching children to sing but that you are moulding their taste. Realizing the amount of commercial trash they meet outside the school, do your utmost to introduce them only to the worthwhile when you have the opportunity. There is plenty of good music which is simple enough and interesting to the child.

Plan your work in advance so that the repertoire is wide. Avoid limiting the songs used to a particular period, and try to have folksong, classical and modern songs all represented in each term's work. Be adventurous about this—always on the look-out for things to use. There are hosts of folksongs—not just the well-known few—of other countries as well as your own. Schubert wrote some six hundred songs—not just 'Who is Sylvia?'—and the art of composition did not die with Mendelssohn.

'GROANERS'

A word about 'groaners'—those unhappy children who seem unable to sing with the rest and spend all their time somewhere down in the bass clef. Not all of them, by any means, are tone-deaf. Many of them have never developed the ability to 'place' the notes which they hear—theirs is perhaps a purely muscular deficiency—and with patience it is possible to rescue them from the depths. Never rebuke a child in this category—above all don't tell him that he can't sing. If you are willing to give the time to it, with careful treatment and a little coaxing, many children who *seem* to be tone-deaf can gradually learn to produce the right notes.

Take such a child to a piano by himself, perhaps at playtime or after school. Play the note A in the treble stave and ask him to sing it. He will probably sing bottom E flat or something similarly outlandish. Many of these children have only one note which they produce whatever you ask for. When he sings his familiar note do not correct him, but identify the note and play it on the piano. Tell him that you are playing the note that he sang and ask him to sing it again. When he has done so, play the note a tone above it and ask him to sing that. *Usually he will be able to do so.* Then explain that you are going to climb up a musical staircase, one step at a time. Getting him to copy each note in turn, play up the first four or five notes of the scale from his starting-point.

In a large number of cases this treatment works. In a series of ten-minute sessions of this kind I have had the pleasure of seeing a number of little boys gradually realize that they *can* sing after all. Once the child has found how to sing up to a fourth or fifth higher than his familiar note, give him regular drills in singing up the scale that far. His confidence will increase rapidly, and you will be able to let him try jumping the interval of a third from his note. By persevering with this sort of thing and gradually increasing the range, the child will learn to sing sufficiently well to join his fellows. And for a boy of ten or eleven who has probably been rebuked or silenced in most singing lessons since he first went to school, this is not unlike a recall from banishment.

6. Instrumental Music

From the first years in the junior school the teacher will be working to ensure that while the music used is simple, the child gradually learns to interpret it for himself from notation. The introduction of simple instrumental music at an early stage will help to bring this about.

Young children need to be active; and percussion work provides an opportunity for disciplined musical activity. The simplest type of percussion work enables children to learn to perform from notation without the complications introduced by changing pitch. The child's whole attention is thus directed to rhythmic considerations, and few children will find the task too difficult. Because the demands made are small, children are able to master the initial stages very quickly, and soon find themselves actually performing. This is an important consideration; and the field of opportunity is a wide one.

The orthodox percussion band developed over a generation ago restricted the instruments in use to a half-dozen miniature replicas of the orchestral percussion group. And while those tiny cymbals, triangles, castanets, tambourines, and the like, are still popular with tots in some schools, the field has subsequently grown considerably beyond that scope—particularly since the experimental work of Carl Orff in Germany became more widely known to the world at large.

Nowadays, it is more usual to find both pitched and unpitched instruments used side by side. Glockenspiel, xylophone, dulcimer, and chime bars are employed on one hand, while the range of the unpitched group itself has been widened to include maracas, washboards, bongo drums, and all manner of exotic instruments, many of which can be home-made, and all of which have a natural appeal for children. Thus, percussion playing has been encouraged to graduate from the junior to the secondary school, with en-

couraging results. Yet, although percussion work has consequently lost its earlier reputation as an activity suitable only
for the toddler, its early stages remain as simple as ever. For the
sake of illustration, let us first consider the introduction of very
simple 'orthodox' percussion work with young children in the
junior school.

UNPITCHED PERCUSSION

It is best to let all the children rehearse their first exercise by
tapping out the rhythm with one finger on the palm of the other
hand. When they can do this, let all the cymbals play it together,
then the drums, and so on. Needless to say, before attempting
percussion music with independent parts for each instrument,
quite a time must be spent on rehearsing all the children in a
single part. This need not be dull. If the teacher designs a simple
rhythmic pattern which can be superimposed on an equally
simple tune, the class can rehearse, even at the earliest stage, while
he plays the piano with them.

A scheme such as this will fit the playing or singing of 'Polly,
put the kettle on':

First line - Triangles: *p* ♩ ♩ | ♩
                         Polly put the kettle on,

Second line - Castanets: *mp* ♩ ♩ | ♩
                         Polly put the kettle on,

Third line - Drums: *mf* ♩ ♩ | ♩
                         Polly put the kettle on, we'll

Fourth line - All: *ff* ♩ ♩ | ♩
                         All   have   Tea!

Something a little more demanding can then be provided by
substituting quavers for the second crotchet.

The first 'pieces' to introduce this work are probably best
fabricated in this way by the teacher, and written on the board.
Limit the children's part to a single rhythmic pattern which is
repeated by each group of instruments in turn. Be careful to
avoid such complications as dotted notes, and, to start with,
keep to tunes which begin on the first beat of the bar. Only

when the whole class is able to perform plenty of these simple things unanimously should the teacher think of introducing independent parts.

When the time comes to take this step, devise a few short 'try-overs' first. Let each group of instruments play its own rhythm *alone*, then let two groups try them simultaneously. Encourage the children to think of this as a tug-of-war in which each part has to 'hold on' to its own music without being put off by what the others are doing. Something simple on these lines is advisable as a first attempt:

1. Drums:
2. Cymbals:
3. Triangles:
4. Tambourines:

When each group has tried to hold its own part against one other group, try three parts in combination before letting them all play together. Once the children have mastered this exercise, take them on a step further by substituting pairs of quavers for some of the crotchets. As a next step, teach the crotchet rest, introducing it to replace a note here and there. But be careful to make these changes in a musical manner. The piece must still sound balanced after you have made these alterations.

The teacher who can extemporize readily will find that this work is made much more enjoyable if he adds a piano part to simple exercises of this kind. With the addition of a concurrent melody, a percussion drill such as this can be repeated several times without seeming monotonous.

Many pieces of music have been written or arranged for percussion, and the teacher will have no difficulty in finding plenty of effective material. In a number of cases arrangements have been made of standard works; but nowadays the aim is more commonly to integrate the use of percussion instruments with the children's own singing or recorder playing, rather than to rely upon the playing of a set piece on the piano by the teacher. And in so far as the children are thus able to be self-supporting musically, this is clearly an advantage.

PITCHED PERCUSSION

Nowadays, too, the wider range of instruments readily available to schools, and the increased musical effect obtained by adding simple parts for chime bars, make even the early stages of this work much more satisfying, as an example will show. Here, the intention is to give individual chime bars to two children, the remainder playing on unpitched instruments or singing the melody. If the prescribed instruments are not all available, the maraca part can be played by using small coffee tins containing a few beads or dried peas; and, at a pinch, chime bars can be improvized from milk bottles tuned by partly filling them with water.

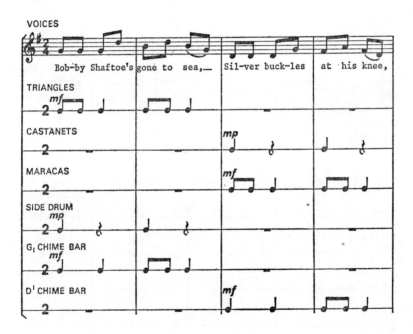

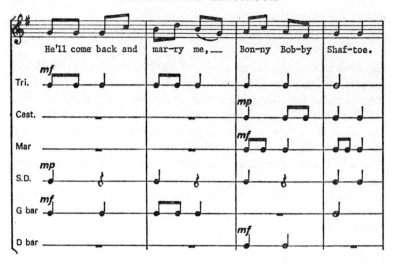

He's my ain for e - ver mair, Bon-ny Bob-by Shaf - toe.

Additional children can enjoy using chime bars in this example, if a group plays the whole triad on G (GBD) or D (DF♯A) instead of just one child playing the single note shown in the score. It would perhaps be wise not to add this extra feature until the performers have dealt competently with the score as it stands. Similarly, two parts for xylophones or dulcimers could also easily be provided in which an 'Alberti bass' part followed the same harmonic scheme as the chime bars:

Two parts of this kind would provide something a little more stimulating (and demanding) for a couple of the more obviously 'musical' children to be found in any class.

One feature to notice in this work is the opportunity it provides for 'expressive' playing. The parts have been liberally supplied with dynamic markings. These should be explained and then observed. Slamming away at instruments with everyone playing as loudly as possible is something to be avoided at all costs. One of the advantages of percussion work is that the players have simple instruments at their disposal which they are able to control completely. The teacher will want to make sure that they do so, not only because the volume of sound will otherwise become intolerable, but also because a musical result is called for—if the children are to acquire insight into musical practice through experience.

Simple arrangements of this kind can be made by the teacher to suit the reading standard of his class. But there are several points to notice before embarking on making these scores—simple though they may be.

First, it is essential to treat the task seriously—as a musical exercise. Scoring for the smallest group of elementary percussion instruments calls for exactly the same basic approach as scoring for a full orchestra. That is, the conjuring up in the mind's ear of the sounds *before* they are set down on the page. It is worse than useless to work out a score on the basis of arithmetic. The arranger must 'hear' the effects which he is writing down.

Secondly, keep the texture of the score 'open': allow plenty of silences, and avoid having everybody biffing away at their instruments all the time. It is as good a musical exercise for the players to have to count out their rests carefully as it is for them to play notes. And the effect will certainly be more musical when the piece is played.

Thirdly, try to get some shape into the scoring. In the example above, two particular points have been considered. With elementary players in mind, the figure ♫ ♩ ('Gone to sea') has been employed consistently throughout in all parts. And the balancing two-bar phrases of the melody have been underlined in the part-writing, so that triangles and side drums, on one hand, and castanets and maracas, on the other, echo each other in two-bar phrases.

If there is a pattern in your mind as you work out your score, the piece will wear better in rehearsal and sound better when it is eventually performed. Above all, the children who play it will be learning more about the nature of music (though perhaps subconsciously) than in many an 'appreciation' lesson.

CREATIVE WORK: WRITING FOR PERCUSSION

When the children have become familiar with playing simple percussion parts of this nature, they should next be shown how to prepare their own scores. Let them work at first as a whole class, yourself taking down their suggestions at the board—criticizing and adapting each proposal until a satisfactory working score has been compiled. After a few joint efforts of this kind have been worked and performed together, the class should then be divided into 'syndicates' of five or six children who, following the same principles, arrange a score of their own—offering and criticizing suggestions jointly until an agreed score is completed. The best scores produced in this way should then be performed and criticized by the class.

The introduction of creative work in music, so engagingly possible on these lines, marks an important stage in the children's musical development, and you are likely to find that thenceforward they begin to adopt a much more positive attitude toward their music lessons. Their efforts to *write* music will automatically encourage a desire to learn more of notation; and much that they learn subsequently will arise from their need to express some musical situation beyond their existing ability to set down on paper.

For this reason, it is a good policy to work towards introducing score arranging as soon as possible in the syllabus. But make sure that the essential groundwork leading up to this stage is not scamped in the process. There is no dearth of published material for the children to perform on percussion instruments; and performance from printed copies of 'real' music has its own attraction for the child. But the advantages of encouraging children to make their own music as well need not be further stressed.

Apart from the 'orthodox' use of percussion instruments as outlined here, more recent developments in school music have employed these instruments, and a wide variety of others too, in freer style, employing a modern musical idiom. This form of activity is especially suited for use with older children in a secondary school—youngsters who consider that they have outgrown the musical fare of junior classes. These developments will be discussed in the next chapter.

CREATIVE WORK: MELODY-WRITING

The introduction of 'pitched' percussion instruments such as the glockenspiel, xylophone, and chime bars, makes possible the extension of creative work to melody-writing. With the help of an instrument, the child's sense of pitch distinction can be usefully developed side by side with vocal work employing sol-fa to complement staff notation.

Merely to distribute pitch-playing instruments to a whole class for vague attempts at composition by trial and error will inevitably produce havoc. But, fortunately, the instruments made today for educational use are customarily fitted with detachable notes; and chime bars themselves can, of course, be issued separately. Thus, it becomes possible for the teacher to limit the child's scope for experiment, so helping him to learn to control those minimal resources more readily. A parallel situation arises in the Art lesson, where a teacher may provide just two or three primary colours, not a complete palette, for a painting exercise.

A study of very young children's own unselfconscious, private singing will show that a common feature of their vocal efforts is the use of the minor third, *soh-me*, with perhaps an occasional rise to *lah*:

The *soh-me* interval consequently appears to provide the best basic material for early attempts at melody-making by the youngest children. The introduction of a third note, *lah*, can quickly be effected, thus widening the scope very considerably.

At this stage, the notes employed can happily be shown on a two-line stave—a device which can later be extended to include further lines only as new notes are introduced, and further lines become essential:

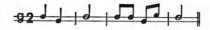

One way of starting this work would be to leave the children free to build 'tunes' for themselves by experiment. The result, although rather noisy, would not prove overwhelming. But after a short period of the trial and error method, children will soon welcome assistance. And perhaps it is better given from the outset.

You can help them to discipline their first efforts by providing them with word patterns to set to music. Limit the first examples to setting individual words—perhaps the names of some of the children themselves. Demonstrate the effect first yourself on a glockenspiel:

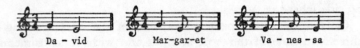

Then go on to something a little more elaborate. The following example, taken a line at a time, would give a young class a reasonably undemanding opportunity, while helping to control their efforts:

> Where's the cat? In the house.
> Look! he's hunting for a mouse.

As a first step in setting these words, let the class tap or clap the normal rhythm of the first line. Then, with their co-operation, write the result on the board:

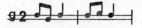

Next, let them attempt to pick out a melody on their three-note instruments to fit that rhythm and suit those words. Something on these lines might well result:

The second line of the words should next be treated in the same way. Working in syndicates of two or three sharing an instrument, the children should first make up their own tunes, and then be helped to write them down. Successful examples can then be examined and played by all.

M.I.C.—6

From this stage, as confidence grows and musical sense develops, the range of notes in use can be slowly enlarged to include, first, the lower *doh*, and then, gradually, the remaining degrees of the scale. Avoid enlarging the range too precipitously. There is plenty of time to complete this work thoroughly. Check before successive instrumental sessions to see how far the children's sense of pitch is developing. When they have grown used to employing *me, soh*, and *lah* on instruments, they should be able to reproduce them vocally. Before adding to that range, make sure that the class can *sing* at sight an easy tune based on those notes. Instrumental and vocal work are best developed side by side wherever possible.

Only when a reasonable proportion of the class can sing a three-note tune of this sort at sight and without instrumental prompting are they really ready to go on to the use of further notes—that is, if you want to develop their aural ability, and are not content merely to let them hammer away at instruments. Finding out which note to hit is not at all the same thing as knowing what each note sounds like. Many competent pianists who are unable to sing a hymn tune at sight will tell you that this is true. This instrumental work is fun for the children; but try to make sure that they are gaining in musical status while they are enjoying it.

Older children embarking on this work for the first time, particularly those in the secondary school, will be able to employ a wider range of notes very quickly. No longer of an age when children sing to themselves as tots do, children in secondary schools will not find the basic interval *soh-me* as advantageous. It will not relate so immediately to their more sophisticated musical experience. Instead, these children can begin by employing the more familiar notes of the common chord, *doh, me, soh*, quickly adding other notes to that range to complete the scale. But in the same way as with the little ones, older children should be encouraged to show that these notes mean something to them aurally, by being invited to sing tunes based on the limited range which they have been using, before adding to that number.

Older children, too, will often find this work more appealing if they are asked to write the *words* themselves before they set out to provide the tunes for them. Once they have worked an example or two of the kind outlined above—though a couplet like 'Where's the cat?' won't do at all in the secondary school—they should be encouraged to set texts of their own devising. Once the tune is complete, it should then be scored for percussion. Higher up the secondary school, those who are fast leaving their childhood completely behind them will no doubt enjoy writing the words and music of their own 'pop' tunes in this way. I have seen this activity introduced and taken up with great zest in one or two schools. By this time the presence of an instrumentalist or two can be assumed in most classes. A guitarist would be a boon, of course. With his expertise to draw on, the rest would quickly find out something about the simple harmonic progressions which such tunes rely on, and be ready to proceed to score their examples on the lines outlined above, but at their own level of ability.

INSTRUMENTAL TUITION, THE SCHOOL ORCHESTRA AND BAND

Most local authorities provide the services of peripatetic instrumental teachers who visit the schools of the area to conduct classes or individual lessons. Quite a wide variety of instruments may be taught in this way in schools; and the foundation of a school orchestra or band can thus be laid. Your County Music Adviser should be approached about the possibility of organizing classes at your school.

Some teachers are unaware of the help which they can obtain from their music adviser. A few appear not to know of his existence or to think of him as someone who wants to interfere. Far from this, the adviser is usually so busy advising and organizing that he will not come to your school unless you ask him to do so. It is a good idea for every young teacher, once he has found his feet in a new school, and has had time to see its possibilities and shortcomings, to invite the adviser to visit the school and discuss plans with him.

Even though you have enrolled promising numbers in your instrumental classes, you will not find the formation of a school orchestra possible overnight. 'Instant' music is something not yet available to us—for better or worse. The classical orchestra depends for its structure upon string players, and these are the very players whose skill only develops slowly; most schools are, very short of violinists capable of playing well enough to appear in public with an orchestra. If you find yourself in the happy position of having a half-dozen good violinists at your disposal, the formation of a school orchestra becomes an immediate possibility. Starting with them plus a piano, and adding whatever other players of reasonable standard happen to be available in the school, a little orchestra can begin rehearsals straight away. As time goes on, other instruments can be added. A double bass would transform the sound of the performance if you can persuade someone to take up the instrument. It is not as difficult to play as other stringed instruments.

If string players of any competence are few and far between, players of wind instruments, on the other hand, can usually be found in some strength in most secondary schools. Even in schools with a strong and long-standing musical tradition, it is not unusual to find six clarinet players for every string player. As a result, differing approaches to the formation of ensembles for school performance are customary nowadays. In some schools, a wind band is much more readily formed than a string-based orchestra. In others, orchestral works are still made the goal, but the orchestration is re-arranged to allow the treble wind instruments to double the violin parts. Each school has to find its own answer to this question.

To start a wind band is not at all difficult, so long as you adopt a sensible attitude to the choice of music in the opening stages. There is, of course, a considerable amount of 'pure' wind music available today—the works of the Gabrielis (Andrea and Giovanni) spring to mind at once. But you will need very competent players to attempt these demanding pieces. They present something to aim towards, rather than an immediate opportunity. Your first pieces should be arrangements which you make to suit the technique of your players. In some schools, when a band is built up from scratch, the first pieces to try the hands of the players will be simple hymn tunes, scored for wind. Elsewhere, some of the simpler organ or virginal pieces will make good material to transcribe. But in almost every case the teacher will have to be prepared to make his own score and parts to suit the players concerned. He must, therefore, learn how to write for transposing instruments—such as the clarinets. A very useful book to have by you for this purpose is Gordon Jacob's *Orchestral Technique*.

Do not think that everything the orchestra or band tries its hand at is necessarily for public, or even for school performance. Wait until your players can present something worth listening to before you put them before an audience. In fact, they will be quite satisfied to work for their own edification and enjoyment in the early stages. Remember that, for a player who has never experienced ensemble work before, even to play a straightforward hymn tune can be quite a thrill. When they can do that, allow them to play for assembly occasionally. Later they can join with the recorders for the carols at Christmas time. On such an occasion the band might well make its first solo performance in a voluntary. When choosing what they should play, make sure that it is something which is well within their power. The simplest music, if well played, is far more rewarding both to audience and players than a more difficult piece which the band cannot quite manage to bring off.

Beside the usual orchestral instruments, there are two other instruments which you may wish to arrange to have taught in classes by visiting teachers. These are the piano and the guitar.

It is only in fairly recent times that serious attempts have been made in schools to teach the piano in classes. The method has the same advantages and disadvantages that apply to instrumental class teaching of any type. In the hands of a competent visitor, the early stages of learning to play the piano can be successfully covered in this way; and many children who might not otherwise have tried their hand at the instrument can be encouraged to begin in class. Once the initial stages are covered, those with any talent will not need to be pressed to continue under individual tuition.

The guitar is very popular with young people today. There is a *mystique* about the instrument, quite apart from its purely musical value. And if a class can be arranged, it is unlikely to want recruits. There are two points for the teacher to note about advertising guitar classes in schools. One is that most youngsters have a very false idea of the initial difficulty of taking up the guitar. It is that 'Instant Music' thing again. The secondhand shops are full of guitars that boys and girls have bought, only to find they cannot just pick them up and start playing straight away. The teacher will wisely emphasize this point to children before they commit their parents to buying them an instrument.

The second point is this. Many youngsters today have a romantic yearning to become pop singers. They have heard over and over again of individuals only a little older than themselves who have actually achieved the miraculous transformation from schoolchild to popular idol. And it is not only the glamour which they find so attractive—it is the money, too. Many children (taking their cue from the adult world) equate success with money. A musical situation which encourages them to do so is one which the music teacher cannot ignore. The matter needs thinking out and airing with the children themselves as they grow older.

The 'Instant Music' point of view itself might well be discussed with older classes as well. There seems little doubt that the attitude which assumes that a guitar can be played without training or practice is closely linked with the attitude which judges merit in music by immediate response. More experienced listeners know that it is only after many hearings that the qualities of great music become apparent. The Radio 1 listener is not brought into contact with music which demands frequent hearing. His musical diet consists much more of things which rely upon immediate impact, then quickly go out of fashion, and are discarded. Matters of this sort should be freely talked about in music lessons with older classes. The teacher who decides to tackle the problem, however, must remind himself that he is discussing with the class the different responses which are called for in listening to different types of music. He is not setting out to condemn one type of music.

RECORDERS

The recorder provides another opportunity for musical activity in junior as well as secondary schools. The subject is too specialized to be dealt with fully in a general treatise of this kind. But here are a few observations which may be of value.

The teacher should realize that before he can teach children to do so, he must be able to play the recorder himself. Breath control, tonguing and intonation are matters that must be demonstrated by a teacher who has himself mastered the technique.

It is not enough to teach fingering from a chart. A carefully graded series of pieces for the children to play should be selected —the first of these employing only the simplest notes, with subsequent pieces gradually adding to the range.

The teacher will have to make an important decision of policy before introducing recorder work. It can either be conducted as a class-group activity or on a voluntary basis. Although it is possible for a school to provide sufficient recorders, there are obvious hygienic objections to children using a borrowed wind-instrument.

Perhaps the best way is to provide a pool of instruments to start with, but to get the children to ask their parents to let them buy their own as soon as possible. A duplicated letter to parents explaining that recorder lessons are to begin, and pointing out the disadvantages of using borrowed instruments, would help to avoid misunderstandings. At the same time, details of the make and size of instrument required could be sent, to ensure that everyone uses an instrument of the same pattern and pitch.

Even though a whole class begins to learn at the same time you cannot expect uniform progress, nor can you get very far with such a large group. Consequently it may prove necessary to continue the work later on a voluntary basis: better still, to start a separate recorder band, drawn from all over the school, for the benefit of those who are making greater headway than their fellows. When this stage is reached, the gradual addition of trebles, tenors, and if possible a bass recorder, for the older and more experienced players, will open the way to the increased musical opportunities provided by playing in consort.

A very considerable range of pieces for unison and many varieties of consort-playing is published for recorders. Every standard of attainment, from the beginner to the advanced player, is catered for. A high proportion of this music has the advantage of being originally written for the instrument. Several good tutors are available, and the teacher who has learned to play himself will have no trouble in finding suitable material for this worth-while activity.

HARMONICAS

The harmonica used to be known as the 'mouth-organ', and as such, received scant attention from serious musicians until the virtuoso performances of Larry Adler led Vaughan Williams to write a concerto for the instrument. Even then, it was difficult for many to dismiss from their minds the concept of the instrument as associated with those tedious chord progressions produced by random, alternate sucking and blowing.

The impression is misleading. The harmonica can be taught as a *melodic* instrument; and many schools have found that boys—who sometimes grow to scorn the recorder—will take to the harmonica more readily for its 'masculine' associations. Taught seriously with the assistance of one of the published tutors, the instrument can be a valuable additional resource in children's music-making. I have listened to mixed consorts of recorders and harmonicas played by junior school children which gave real pleasure. The combination of tone colour produced was most acceptable—strongly reminiscent, indeed, of a chamber organ—and the instruments complemented each other very happily. One of the available tutors allows recorders and harmonicas to be taught side by side—a useful consideration in a mixed school.

The special harmonicas produced for school use comprise a diatonic instrument for beginners, and a chromatic instrument for more advanced players. Both types can be used in combination for ensemble work. A useful collection of performing material is published, some details of which will be found in the lists at the end of this book.

7. The School, and Music Today

In recent years, more and more people have become aware that, while thinking of themselves as music-lovers, they knew next to nothing of the music of their own day.

A book of this kind is not the place to undertake the lengthy discussion needed even to attempt to explain how that state of affairs should have come about. But the music teacher who takes his responsibilities seriously will be unwilling to turn his back on a situation so problematical and challenging.

It is tempting to dismiss the matter in these pages with a brief injunction to the teacher, advising him to keep abreast of current musical developments, and not to forget to include the work of living composers among the pieces which he introduces to his pupils. But one has seen advice of that sort misfire too often to succumb to the temptation.

Sometimes, such advice fails because it is ignored; but it fails at least as often because the case has been overstated. A few of the articles and lectures addressed to teachers on this subject have hinted that a liking for the music written before this century is somehow reprehensible; others have come near to asserting that because a composer happens to be alive today, he must be a good composer. A teacher may find himself losing his self-confidence as a result of such aggressive handling; but he is unlikely to be persuaded to change his ways thereby.

Yet, there is no doubt that teachers of music must feel at least the same measure of responsibility towards current events in their own field as do teachers of, say, art. And it is perhaps by examining the parallel a little more closely that progress may be made.

THE EXAMPLE OF THE ART LESSON

For a generation or more, one of the most enviable features of the art lesson has been the way in which teachers have been able to distribute the necessary materials to children, and then let them start straight away to paint creatively. Perhaps the teacher would suggest a title, or simply ask the children to design a pattern. In either case, they were able, once they had learned to manage a brush, to begin painting spontaneously. Sometimes the result was rather a mess; at other times, aided by the teacher's helpful criticism, children produced impressive results; but in every case, it is suggested, the children concerned were able to enjoy the satisfaction of personal creation, and, incidentally, to learn something of the sensations experienced by a painter—and hence about painting itself.

It was often with a feeling approaching envy that the music teacher regarded the creative aspect of his colleague's opportunities in the art room. If only, he would say to himself, if only I could get my classes to express their own musical ideas with the same freedom. To do so, of course, seemed out of the question. Whereas with painting you appeared to need only the materials and the imagination to be able to 'create', with music you also required the ability to employ a complicated system of notation, and a knowledge of harmony into the bargain. To acquire both skills was the work of years—by which time, the spontaneity of childhood would have passed.

Yet, if further thought is given to the matter, it will be realized that an earlier type of art lesson required of pupils that they should become adept at drawing, shading, and perspective, and should have studied the brush technique of the great painters, before ever they were let loose at a canvas. By that time, too, the spontaneity of childhood must have passed.

And so, it appears, art teachers decided that the average child should be allowed to by-pass the traditional training in technical skills, and be allowed to express his own ideas in his own way, developing his skill and his insight by doing so. It was no accident that this development in the teaching of art in schools took place at a time when painters themselves were abandoning traditional attitudes and techniques in their own work.

The music teacher today is in a position to follow that example from the art lesson by allowing the child to by-pass, for the time being, the traditional elements in formal musical education, and to proceed directly to experiment with sound. As with the art lesson—where the techniques of contemporary painters provided both the example and the means—so in the music lesson today, current practice in musical composition demonstrates both the possibilities of pure sound arrangement and a simple method of notating the result. Today, children can begin to perform and then to compose in the classroom without a long period of initial training. Needless to say, they will be able to do these things only at their own level; they will not write like Beethoven or Palestrina, any more than in the art lesson they painted like Titian or Canaletto. Significantly enough, however, their compositions will often resemble Stockhausen as much as their paintings resemble Paul Klee.

MUSIC-MAKING IN A NEW IDIOM

However simple a classroom activity may be, before expecting children to adopt it they must become familiar with what it involves. The new and simple forms of notation employed in this work may be introduced to them step by step, through actual performance. A start can be made by employing a few of the symbols used to denote the *length* of sounds, for instance in the notation used by George Self:

•	an abrupt sound
⌒	an undamped sound
•—	a sustained sound
∿	a shake, or trill

Empty space on the page implies silence. Pulse is irregular and not dependant upon barlines. Distance on the page indicates the relative speed. The conductor (at first the teacher) controls the performance by a gesture at the numbered 'barlines'.

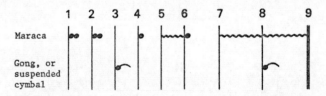

This little exercise for two players could be performed several times by different players in a variety of different ways—the conductor deciding just how it should sound. It could even be played without a conductor, once the players had found what was required of them.

Further modification (and improvement) would result from the introduction of different levels of volume—thus introducing the children to the symbols *f* (bar one) *p* (bar two) and ◁══ (bar seven).

A host of short 'pieces' of this kind could be prepared employing more instruments, but only this material, the children soon being ready to compose them for themselves. From mutual criticism and the teacher's comments when their pieces are performed, children quickly learn to control the material at their disposal more effectively. This work helps them, that is to say, to learn to *listen* as well as play.

At a later stage, differences in pitch can be introduced. Teachers who have prepared themselves for this work positively will realize, from acquaintance with music of the present day, that the character of pitch relationship called for is chromatic; that if the note D is followed by, say, F sharp and A, a musical anachronism will be produced. They will choose, instead, to employ a group of notes which does not produce an out-of-period 'flavour'—for instance, D, G sharp, and C sharp.

The chosen notes are then best made available to the children, at first, by distributing to the performers the individual chime bars concerned. Notation is arranged spatially—in this case for three chime bars:

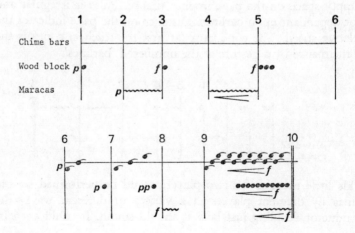

More elaborate scores, designed to employ all the members of a class—some working in groups—and involving a much wider range of instruments, can be built up as the work proceeds. Some of these scores will resemble the example given, in the sense that they will be 'abstract' patterns of sound; others may well be produced as 'programme' pieces. I have heard some fascinating examples of children's own composition in this field. In one instance, a class of secondary girls, working together as a syndicate and pooling their ideas, produced a miniature sound track for an imaginary film in which the drama of a fly caught in a spider's web was shown. The result was highly effective and showed how imaginatively children will approach this type of challenge. Many school plays would lend themselves to the performance of incidental music composed especially by the children in this way, and taped beforehand.

An even happier use of this work would be to allow the children to employ it in conjunction with their more 'orthodox' efforts at melody-writing and scoring, to produce a school opera. Ideally, in such a case, the plot would allow for deliberate contrast between the two different styles of writing. For instance, in a fairy-tale libretto, the supernatural aspect would lend itself to the use of the new idiom, while the human element would employ ordinary 'tunes'. Witches, ogres, and fairies would use stylized speech; human characters would sing. The task would be a considerable one, but children who had been following a stimulating course including both types of creative work would not find it beyond their capability—especially not if the task were shared by several classes in the school.

Some young composers have begun to produce scores for school use, employing new techniques similar to those outlined. Many of these new pieces are for groups of simple percussion instruments. The following extract, however, is the opening of a piece which calls for nothing more than hands and voices—*plus* imaginative direction from the teacher:

Sound Patterns 1 *

for voices and hands

Bernard Rands

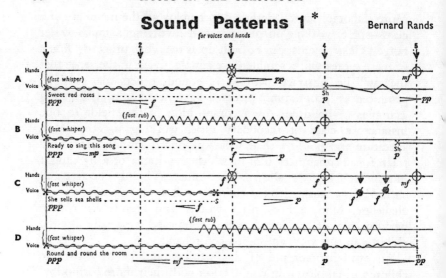

Performance is controlled by a gesture from the conductor at each of the numbered arrows at the top of the score. The symbols employed are self-explanatory (once one has overcome an initial surprise at their failure to resemble standard notation) and pitch variation is shown simply by rise and fall on the page. On first encountering a score of this kind, it is a good idea to examine its make up carefully, and then set oneself to *imagine* the combination of sounds which would result in actual performance.

One important feature in this new field is the amount of freedom which it allows to the performer. Pitch and rhythm are not laid down inflexibly; the performers contribute a personal element to even the simplest of these pieces. As their experience grows, the individual performers are encouraged to increase that improvisatory element, until, at a later stage, they are able to create the whole texture of the music for themselves.

When that stage is reached, the scores employed may provide some general guidance as to the melodic and rhythmic outline to be followed. For instance, if the score includes a shape of this

kind,   the implication is that a melodic figure follow-

ing that general outline is called for—perhaps something on these

* Reproduced with the permission of Universal Edition (London) Ltd.

lines: 𝄞 ♪ ♪ But the player is left free to interpret the detail for himself.

At a still later stage, when the performers have grown less inhibited and are able to extemporize short figures readily, they can even dispense with diagrammatic guidance as to *what* they are to play, their contribution being perhaps governed only by a direction as to *when* they should play.

Here is an example of a score which enables older and more experienced performers to work in this way. It is the opening of a rather longer score by George Self, the pioneer of this whole new field of musical activity in our schools, and it is included here with his permission:

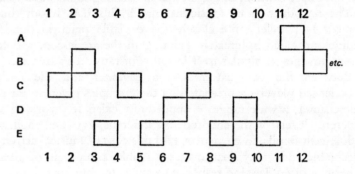

The most surprising feature of this unusual score is that it contains no notes whatsoever; not even the instruments which are to perform have been specified. Everything except the 'form' of the piece is left to be decided by the performers and conductor. The letters in the margin represent the individual instruments, or groups of instruments, to take part; the areas 'blocked in' show *when* each should play. Just *what* they will improvise is left to them to decide.

First attempts at performance from such a score may well be chaotic. But it is through the criticism of those first attempts that the performers learn to master the material at their disposal through self-imposed discipline.

After a first trial run at a score of this kind, the teacher must invite the performers to criticize the result. They will probably admit, readily enough, that it was a muddle. Prompted by the teacher, they will quickly discover that the muddle was due to the use of too much material—too many sounds unrelated to each other. Given a second chance to play the same score, they will begin to learn to *listen* to each other while awaiting their own entries, so as to be able to cause motifs and figures introduced in one part to be echoed or answered in another. Once the importance of 'organizing' their own improvisation in this way has thus been realized, such a group of players will have been prompted to learn something of a universal musical truth—that economical use of material is an artistic criterion; and that composers tend to make new use of existing material rather than introduce new ideas throughout the whole course of a score. The discovery will have a bearing not only on their work in the field of improvisation, but upon that in listening to music as well.

The introduction of music-making in this new idiom thus appears to parallel quite closely the enviable practical opportunities provided by creative painting in the art lesson, and to afford advantages similar to it in terms of musical awareness.

Between the two extremes—the beginner and the fairly experienced player—represented by the examples given so far in this chapter, a wide range of opportunity exists for working at different levels with children of different age and ability. Adolescent pupils, in particular, find this type of musical activity acceptable in a way that makes possible a renewal of their otherwise often flagging response to music teaching in school.

The teacher who wishes to learn more of the detail of this new aspect of school music will find a more adequate introduction to the subject in George Self's own publication, *New Sounds in Class*, which provides not only an authoritative step-by-step account of how to proceed with this work, but also the material to cover an extended course of lessons.

Another resource which the modern music teacher is learning to value is the tape-recorder—employed as a device to transform and mingle sounds. Making a composite sound-track, with elements which have first been recorded separately—some of them at half or double speed—can prove a fascinating and instructive activity for older children in particular. Work on these lines, begun at the simplest level and gradually becoming more adventurous, can both help to develop young people's aural sensitivity and provide them with opportunities for imaginative self-expression. Once again, it is perhaps in conjunction with a performance by the dramatic society that their interest in 'electronic' music can first be captured.

The teacher who decides to introduce activities such as these in his school may well find that the children's response is enthusiastic—so much so that he may be led to devote a large proportion of his time with classes of this work. Such a teacher will be wise to recall what has been said elsewhere in this book about the necessity of keeping a balance between the variety of aspects within an ideal music course.

Few teachers in these days would accept as desirable an interpretation of their task which limited them to the teaching of songs by rote. They would no doubt claim that, with all the opportunities which developments in music-teaching now afford, such an interpretation of their rôle was too narrow. It would be disappointing if the discovery of a new and exciting aspect of school music-teaching merely led to a new dogmatism and narrowness of outlook.

Over-enthusiastic teachers of Tonic Sol-fa in the past produced a situation in which their pupils later found themselves unable to read standard works printed in staff notation. A similar situation could result from exclusive attention to this new type of music-making in schools. As it stands, the notation employed in this work does not automatically lead to an understanding of staff notation; and the characteristic intervals of its chromatic instrumental idiom are too difficult for average children to master either aurally or vocally. It is therefore essential to maintain both singing and the use of standard notation in other parts of the music course, if the children concerned are to become 'educated' in music.

If this new style music-teaching is developed in isolation, it can all too easily be made to appear to contradict the traditional aims of the music lesson. But these dangers will be avoided if the teacher sets out to integrate this new *branch* of school music into a well-balanced syllabus aimed, as we have already argued, towards helping the child to become musically articulate, literate, and responsive.

So long as this work is developed as part of such a total scheme, its contribution to the vitality of the music course can be both considerable and immediate. In no other way yet devised is the child able to experience the sensations of musical creation so readily; or to come into contact with the idiom of current music so directly. But remember that for him to do so, he must be guided by a teacher who is himself familiar with that idiom. The scores which children are invited to perform and create in this work will 'make sense' only if the teacher's ear is adequately trained to criticize and direct them.

To return to the analogy with the art lesson, a teacher whose acquaintance with painting stops short at Gainsborough will be less able to criticize a child's efforts helpfully than one who has acquired knowledge of and sympathy with developments in painting during the present century. The music teacher whose world comes to an end with Brahms will not find himself able to develop this work profitably in his school. The children he should be guiding will prove to be more 'contemporary' than he is. Moreover, much of his teaching in other branches of the music syllabus will tend to suffer, too, for the same reason.

This chapter therefore ends, as it might well have begun, by advising the teacher to keep abreast of current musical trends and events, and not to forget to include the work of living composers among the pieces which he introduces to his pupils.

8. Other Musical Activities

Never overtax children's listening capacity. If you talk too long, much of what you say will begin to pass them by; if you play music to them for too long, the same thing will happen. Because of this consideration, the modern music-teacher is more disposed to help children make their musical discoveries through the music which they perform themselves than through invitations to listen to others performing. But recorded music can still make a valuable contribution to musical education if it is carefully selected, skilfully introduced, and not over-employed.

LISTENING TO MUSIC

Music which reaches children from a loudspeaker, whether by means of radio or record-player, lacks the advantages of 'live' performance. Because of that limitation it cannot be expected to hold the child's attention for long. In the junior school, recorded music intended to develop 'active' listening should not last more than three or four minutes at a stretch. With the youngest children even this is too long. The small 45 rpm record is much more appropriate in length for most school purposes than the long-playing record.

In the secondary school, children who have learned something about the music itself first, may be able to listen for longer at a time. But with them, too, it is very easy to produce boredom and inattention when your aim has been to do the opposite. Don't overlook the simple expedient of introducing them to snippets of the music before they hear it all. This preliminary experience will give them 'milestones' to range between. And after you have made your initial points and illustrated them at the piano, let the class hear these passages played orchestrally from the recording itself.

The problem here is 'finding' the appropriate spot on the record. One of the advantages of the obsolete 78 rpm record was that it could be marked with a wax crayon for this purpose without causing damage; but l.p. records are far more sensitive. Not only must they not be marked in this way, but even to set down the needle midway through a turning disc is likely to ruin the recording.

One way of dealing with the problem is, first, to identify the position of the required excerpt by measuring the distance from the centre of the record with a calibrator. (You can make a simple one yourself with a narrow strip of card marked in millimetres along the edge, and with a hole at one end to fit over the central post.) Once it has been located, when the passage concerned is next required, stop the turn-table, turn down the volume control completely, and set down the needle carefully just before the groove in question. Then restart the turn-table, and, as the record spins regularly, turn up the volume control again. This method avoids damaging the surface, and also avoids the 'moaning' effect otherwise produced as the disc gains speed.

A more professional method is to tape the required extracts in advance. Over a period of time a useful library of recorded thematic material can be built up and indexed in this way. In either case, details of the extracts and their location should be marked on the record sleeve concerned, for future use.

PRESENTATION OF RECORDED MUSIC

Never allow yourself to underestimate the amount of careful preparation required before you are ready to present a recording in the classroom sufficiently attractively to capture children's attention. The fact that the gramophone company has taken the trouble to provide an extensive blurb on the record sleeve does not reduce your own responsibility in that direction. It is essential for the teacher to know thoroughly the music which he intends to present to a class. He should be sufficiently familiar with it, for instance, to know just what is coming next as the piece proceeds. In certain types of music, a word or a look from the teacher while the music is actually playing will be of value in helping the listeners to follow what is going on. Do not feel guilty about making an occasional brief verbal comment during the playing of a record if you feel that it will help the class in this way. It is something, however, which you can only do if you really know the music.

In almost every department of music-teaching there is a grave risk that the teacher will be tempted to teach *facts about music*, instead of teaching music. It is a hazard apt to occur, as we have seen, in teaching notation; it is equally likely to arise—if the teacher is unwary—where the presentation of music for listening is concerned.

Therefore, before you play a recording to a class, no matter how familiar its title, or how well you know the dates of the composer's birth and death, play the piece over to yourself, and make yourself listen to it as if it were entirely fresh. Listen to it analytically. Have a scrap of paper at your side, and jot down each feature of the music as it strikes you. With programme music it may be descriptive details and features of orchestration which capture your attention; with absolute music, perhaps the formal structure, a repeated figure, or some ingenuity in development will catch your ear. By making a note of such happenings as they occur, you will find that you are able to compile a useful commentary on the piece which will act as the basis of your lesson notes. Each time you do this, you are stimulating your teaching faculties as a musician; and if on a subsequent hearing you repeat the process with the score open before you, further points for your commentary will almost certainly become apparent as you listen. It is in this way that you will find yourself increasingly able to detect 'teaching points' in almost any of the music suitable for presentation in the classroom.

Remember, too, that when you play a recording for a class, you should be *seen to be* listening to it yourself. The reactions of a roomful of children to the progress of a piece of music played for their edification depend far more upon their unconscious reaction to the changing expression on their teacher's face, as he listens with them, than many teachers ever realize. Once this fact is appreciated, you will see how important it is that you should not only listen with your class, but that you should be careful to let your reactions become just that shade more obvious to them. Your own face can become one of your visual aids.

TELEVISION AND RADIO LESSONS

Broadcast music lessons on both sound and television have much to offer—especially to schools with little musical experience and hence limited equipment. But to obtain the best results the children must be prepared beforehand by the teacher, and, once the broadcast is over, many things are likely to need further explanation which can only be given on the spot by someone who knows the children concerned. Very attractively designed pamphlets are published for children to use in following these lessons, as well as detailed teachers' notes published well in advance. These publications enable the teacher to anticipate each lesson and prepare the children to derive the greatest benefit from it.

CORRELATION WITH OTHER SUBJECTS

By consulting with his colleagues, the music teacher can often arrange that the children's songs, as well as the music they listen to, have a special bearing on the work they are doing in other subjects. If they have been hearing about the Battle of Agincourt in their history lesson, teach them that same week the *Agincourt Song*—'Our King went forth to Normandy'; link up the story of Bonny Prince Charlie with *The Road to the Isles*. Older children reading a Shakespeare play, or the younger ones meeting Lamb's *Tales from Shakespeare*, can learn some of the songs from the plays—certainly those reading *A Midsummer Night's Dream* ought to hear some of Mendelssohn's incidental music in their next music lesson. *Marching through Georgia* belongs to General Sherman's exploits in the American Civil War; *Lilliburlero* to James II and the Orangemen; Handel's *Firework Music* and *Water Music* help to make the social scene in Georgian England more real. Recorded extracts—the 'Christmas' music from *Messiah*, or the 'Plague' choruses from *Israel in Egypt*—can link up nicely with scripture lessons. Many of the countries studied in geography lessons have fascinating folksongs and vigorous, exotic national dances which will appeal readily to children—especially if the music lesson follows up the geography lesson promptly.

There is a fine opportunity here for the teacher with initiative who is prepared to plan ahead and go to some trouble to make his work effective. He will find that correlated work of this kind is doubly effective, and will often win the musical interest of many of those children who otherwise fail to respond. Besides this, it helps a music specialist to keep a sense of perspective and to know more of the children themselves. It is fatal for a subject teacher to think that the children have nothing else to do apart from his own subject—yet this is not an uncommon frame of mind for a teacher to adopt.

PRIVATE RECORDINGS

An expert performance of something which they have tried to perform themselves lets children hear music which they know *from the inside*; it also helps them to assess standards, and to learn self-criticism. Remember, too, the advantages of letting children hear *themselves* perform. In these days this is no longer a luxury.

The tape-recorder, used indiscriminately, can become a prodigal time-waster and nuisance in the classroom. But an occasional recording of children's performances can be of great value in helping them to assess their own standards. It can also help to stimulate in them the sense of 'rising to an occasion'—a valuable quality to promote in a school where indifference may perhaps have been allowed to develop over the music.

From time to time, many schools mount musical performances which have called for unusual effort. Such events deserve preservation; and it is worthwhile securing the services of an expert to produce a disc on such an occasion. Provided that the standard of performance is sufficiently high to justify the undertaking, the sale of the records will usually cover the expense involved in producing them.

Never lose sight of the fact that a 'real' recording of a school's own musical performance, especially if it is professionally produced with a smart printed label, can provide a remarkable boost for that school's musical morale. Headmaster, parents, and children alike will be inclined to hold the school's musical activities in higher esteem—so long as the record is worth listening to.

HOUSE MUSIC COMPETITIONS

In secondary schools which are organized on a house basis, an inter-house music competition increases incentive as well as providing an entertainment for the whole school. The child who is both musical and good at games will welcome a further opportunity of working for the prestige of his house. One who is not good at games, but who can play or sing, will be glad to find a way of making up for a deficiency of which he is no doubt very conscious.

Let each house work under a senior who will be responsible for selecting his teams and supervising their rehearsals. The teacher should be prepared to give advice on the choice of music and matters affecting rehearsals, but as a general rule, he should encourage each representative to be responsible for the preparation of his house's entry. Each house team should have one rehearsal with the teacher shortly before the competition takes place.

Teams should be entered to sing, and there should be two or three solo instrumentalists from each house. In addition, teams to undertake musical dictation and sight-reading should take part, but their efforts should be judged privately before the day of the competition, and the points scored credited to each house on a notice-board. Aim later to include an ensemble team from each house. It is unlikely to be possible at first, but is a much more valuable test and more typical of the school's musical activity than solo performance.

It is advisable to hold a semi-final for the soloists, and, in the case of a large school with many houses, perhaps for the choirs as well. The finals should not last longer than an hour. They should be held before the whole school, and it will add considerably to the value of the event if you can persuade a local musical big-wig to undertake the judging. Avoid doing it yourself if you can. A scoreboard should be erected on which the points are displayed as soon as each event has been judged. The atmosphere on such an occasion as the scores mount can be quite as tense as that more customarily associated with the cricket ground.

Get the judge to say something encouraging to those taking

part, and to the school as a whole for their attention, before presenting the trophy; but reserve his detailed comments for the candidates' ears alone. He can either speak to them together afterwards, or, better still, write a brief report on each performance for the performer to read for himself.

COMBINED SCHOOL MUSIC FESTIVALS

Annual occasions for all the schools in an area to come together to make music are commonly arranged nowadays. Usually, all the junior schools meet on a particular day while the secondary schools come together on another. As a rule, an agreed song programme is arranged by a representative committee well in advance, allowing all the schools time to learn the music independently. On the day of the festival all then combine in its performance under a visiting conductor. Sometimes in addition to this, every school prepares one or two pieces of its own choice to sing or play before the assembled children for *written* comment by the conductor-adjudicator. This feature can be very instructive, both for the teachers and the children, as each school in turn performs its chosen pieces.

On such occasions a public concert comprising a selection of the combined items is usually held in the evening for the benefit of the parents of the children taking part. When well managed and enthusiastically supported, these festivals can prove of value to all concerned—besides being good for public relations. They are to be preferred to competitive festivals—where an element of rivalry between schools can easily be over-stimulated, and where the less musically developed schools are unlikely to be willing to expose their limitations by taking part.

CONCERTS FOR SCHOOLS

A few local authorities provide special orchestral concerts for children. I believe it is very easy to over-estimate the value of taking coach-loads of children, chosen haphazardly, to concerts of this kind. There is such an atmosphere of the outing about the whole thing: the escape from school, the coach-ride, the imposing size of the hall—all these exciting things fill the child's mind and virtually intoxicate him. The music, as far as he is concerned, is eclipsed by the events and things surrounding it. That is, unless he is already a *musical* child.

I have watched a hall full of children from a balcony on such an occasion. They arrived in the hall highly excited, and spent the time until the concert began examining the hall and exchanging vigorous greetings with children from other schools in adjacent blocks of seats. The first piece played interested them considerably. They enjoyed watching the conductor and the activities of the players.

After this came a series of demonstrations of various instruments in the orchestra. While an instrument was being explained to them, most of the children followed the speaker quite keenly, and when an odd note or two was played, to demonstrate some point of construction or technique, they were delighted. But when the player proceeded to cap this by playing a piece of music, most of the assembly—boys and girls—lapsed into inattention—either falling half-asleep or turning to clandestine mischief. As the concert proceeded their attention flagged further, and long before the end they had had enough.

A musical experience of this kind is probably only really valuable for a child who has already shown pronounced musical tendencies. And so long as the audience on such an occasion is made up of children selected for their obvious musicality, the venture is laudable. Such children are invariably electrified at first hearing in the flesh orchestral works formerly known to them only from recordings or broadcasts. But for the child who shows no such musical aptitude—whether because it is unawakened or naturally deficient—I believe that concerts of this kind are unlikely to produce the hoped-for results. It is something like throwing a non-swimmer in at the deep end to teach him the elements of the breast stroke. *Sometimes* it works.

Apart from the immense artificialities of the occasion already referred to, such concerts are bound to last too long for children with limited musical awareness. For these children—and they represent a sizeable proportion if not a large majority in most schools—the answer must be different. They should be given the opportunity of seeing and hearing instruments, but in their own schools. Not a whole symphony orchestra—for that presents not only an economic impossibility but an emotional surfeit. Instead let them meet two or three of the instruments at a time.

These can be examined and demonstrated at reasonably close quarters and in familiar surroundings. The experience will be real, and not part of fantasy. After each instrument has been shown and played, a few short pieces should be played in combination—the whole thing lasting little longer than an ordinary lesson. Many education authorities arrange visits of this kind. Once again, the music adviser will answer your enquiries.

9. Some General Considerations

The layout of this book may unintentionally have encouraged its readers to suppose that the teaching of singing, notation, instrumental work, and appreciation, are fields to be developed in isolation. The book will have failed in its purpose if that impression is allowed to continue. While it is a convenience to treat each of those topics separately in writing about them here, in the classroom the various aspects of music must be integrated and allowed to interact.

INTEGRATED MUSIC TEACHING

If the teacher goes about his work with the right viewpoint, every part of every music lesson will be concerned with musical appreciation. To regard the teaching of 'appreciation' as limited to those occasions when recordings are played is absurd—but not uncommon. When children first sing the 'Missing Note Game', or later try their hands at elementary composition or arranging, they are developing powers of musical appreciation. When they play or sing with enjoyment, they are learning to appreciate music. They are also learning to interpret musical notation. Indeed, it is in the course of those activities that new details of notation will best be introduced.

The thoughtful reader will have observed that the chapter on 'Teaching Notation' in this book treats only the earliest stages of the syllabus. That limitation is deliberate. The chapter's purpose is to demonstrate the way in which each topic may be *introduced*. Its further intention is to emphasize the wisdom of teaching notation, not as a series of symbols to be committed to memory, but as the examination of certain simple aural sensations, followed by explanation of the way in which musicians indicate them on the page. When children have learned—as they easily can in their very first lesson on the subject—to distinguish between the simplest symbols, they are at once able to *employ* them in performance.

Once that initial stage has been reached, further symbols may be introduced as the need for them arises. Thus, the teaching of notation will not be allowed to become an end in itself—the tiresome study of an apparently pointless skill for its own sake—but will serve a clear purpose, as the children themselves will quickly realize.

As a general rule, lessons should not be planned to cover only one aspect of music. There should not be alternately 'Singing' lessons, 'Theory' lessons, 'Musical Appreciation' lessons. Instead, most music lessons should allow for a refreshing variety of activity; and the teacher should have a finger on the pulse of the class so as to decide when a change of activity would be beneficial.

In planning lessons on these lines, see that the various elements included bear some clear relationship to each other—the work in notation arising naturally out of the music performed; the music listened to being chosen to relate to a topic already under discussion. Avoid allowing the lesson to proceed in a series of jerks, with changes of activity seeming to occur pointlessly. When a lesson seems to be disjointed the class may be left at its end with a feeling that nothing worthwhile has been achieved.

This recommendation should not, however, be taken to mean that every music lesson *must* include work under all the headings mentioned. It will sometimes happen that, in order to deal adequately with some tricky or absorbing point, the bulk, or even the whole of a lesson will be required. At other times abandoning a particular topic would mean losing the interest of the class. Don't be afraid to depart from the planned lesson you have prepared if your class is obviously ready to spend longer on one topic or activity, or if some point arises—perhaps through a child's question—which calls for attention then and there. The ability to exercise judgement as to when to make a change of material, according to class response, is part of the equipment of the competent teacher.

THE TEACHER AND HIS CLASS

The first pages of this book were concerned with the importance of a right attitude in the teacher. The matter can hardly be over-emphasized, for every class where music is badly taught is a nursery for musical allergy and indifference. Often enough, shortcomings in music-teaching are due less to a teacher's musical inadequacy than to his mishandling of the children. The last pages of this book are therefore devoted to the consideration of some basic teaching techniques.

Young teachers have usually been trained to believe that the key to success in the classroom lies in interesting the children. This is certainly the case. An ill-prepared, dull lesson cannot be expected to succeed; but one that is well prepared and imaginative can also fail if the teacher does not secure the attention of the class before introducing it.

Before embarking upon any lesson, make sure that the class has settled down. In some schools music lessons are given in a particular room where each class assembles after making its way from another part of the building. When this is so, the teacher must obviously supervise and control a definite settling-down process before launching into his lesson. But even when no such migration is involved, and the class remains in the same room, the teacher should realize that the children come to him fresh from an encounter with another subject. As a result, particularly if this has been one which they have found stimulating, the class is likely to need some moments of relaxation—and perhaps even chatter—before they are ready to adjust themselves to another period devoted to a different topic.

Dealing with this interim calls for judgement and common-sense. Use the time involved to see that books are put away, while your own material is distributed, the board cleaned, and apparatus and instruments are moved into place. Be business-like, but do not make unreasonable demands for silence during these moments. Only when everything is ready need you call for attention.

This first call for attention is a critical test in the establishment of discipline. Good class-control springs from attention to detail. When you have told a class to pay attention, *wait for the instruction to be carried out by everyone.* And be prepared to single out individuals who do not comply, repeating your previous instruction with meaningful firmness. Young teachers who 'have discipline problems' have usually brought this about by failing to observe this basic rule. An inexperienced teacher is inclined to believe that because he has given an instruction he can assume that it will be carried out; that he has magically acquired the *aura* of 'a teacher' to which the children will equally magically respond. Or, what is worse, he will not allow himself to note that his instruction has not been obeyed, because he is uncertain how he should deal with the disobedient. He therefore fails to check that his instruction has been obeyed *by every individual*. It is only necessary to give three or four instructions which are not fulfilled by everyone in the class to create the impression in the children's minds that you do not mean what you say. And once that impression exists, class control can develop into a real problem, only to be solved slowly and painfully. More and more of the class will come to ignore what you say, and to feel that they can do so with impunity. This being so, things will only deteriorate if the teacher is so unwise as to turn to threats. Yet often it is the very teacher whose inexperience has made him fail to ensure that his initial instructions are obeyed, who later utters threats which he lacks the will, or the authority, to carry out.

Remove the cause of bad discipline from the outset by giving clear instructions, and learning to check that every child has obeyed them. With an habitually unruly class, it may even be necessary to devote considerable time at the start of a first lesson to establishing control in this way. If this is so, do not regard this as time wasted. Delay the introduction of your prepared lesson until you have secured everyone's attention. Then plunge straight into the matter of the lesson. Take particular pains, with a 'difficult' class, to present your opening material as attractively as possible. The critical point that you have to make to them is that your lessons are *worth* listening to, your class activities are *worth* joining in.

Once attention has been secured, it must be held. This is where the preparation of the lesson as something vital and interesting is of such importance. But there is a great difference between an interesting lesson and an interesting *lecture*. Children's attention is best held by allowing—nay, causing them to participate. In the average music lesson there are so many opportunities for the children to take an active part—in singing and music-making of one kind or another—that it is tempting to assume that once the teacher decides to expound some point of musical theory, or to give some account of a piece of music to be played, that there is no further need for the class to do more than listen to him. This is a mistake. It is generally a good principle not to tell children something which they can be induced to tell you. In other words, active participation can be stimulated by skilful questioning.

Asking questions in the classroom is by no means the foolproof matter that it appears to some. It is all too easy to ask ambiguous questions. In framing a question, the teacher should consider what answer he expects to receive. In your first lessons it is a good idea to *write out*, for your own guidance, the actual wording of the questions to be posed. This safeguard will ensure careful preparation on your part, and the avoidance of ambiguity. Wrong answers from children should not always be automatically rejected without comment. Often a child who has given a wrong answer can be encouraged to think again, or helped to adjust his answer step by step by means of further questioning, until the right answer is forthcoming. Good questioning technique avoids snubbing the child who has answered incorrectly; bad questioning technique causes more and more of the class to lose self-confidence, and results in smaller numbers wanting to follow the course of the lesson. Sometimes, individual children will succumb to the temptation to provide silly answers. This calls for judgement in the teacher. Occasionally the child who is simply 'showing off' must be gently snubbed; sometimes his silly answer should be analysed—*by him*. The rest of the class will be inclined to side with the teacher against merely foolish individuals once their silliness has been exposed. But most usually, foolery of this kind is best passed over without comment.

When asking questions, refrain from the common habit of allowing the class to call out answers. Insist upon raised hands if you mean to secure and keep control. But once the practice of raised hands is established, remember sometimes to question children whose hands are not raised. The less bright are not too dull to realize that they can often hibernate unprovoked and free from mental stress simply by refraining from raising their hands —if you let them. Widen the field of attention and participation in your class by seeking answers to your questions from children who do not think that they can answer. It is nearly always possible by careful questioning, a step at a time, to winkle out correct answers from diffident children who have not raised their hands. Every time this happens, at least one child in your care has gained encouragement, and the tone of your teaching has correspondingly improved.

The level of interest shown by a class of children is very often a reflection of the teacher's own apparent interest in what he is presenting. Instead of speaking *at* a class, speak *to* them as a group of individuals—and in a way which indicates that you yourself find the topic of great interest. This does not involve caricatured enthusiasm, but perfectly normal interest in your subject. You are presumably an enthusiast; do not veil your enthusiasm. Act and speak naturally, but keep alert.

It is unfortunately common to find that an inexperienced teacher does not realize that he spends a great deal of time speaking (apparently) to the back wall of the classroom in a numb voice devoid of any variety of pace and pitch. It is essential to create an impression of addressing each child individually. This is done, quite simply, by allowing your glance to travel around from one pair of eyes to another throughout the *whole* class as you are speaking. It is only necessary for eyes to meet for a split second, but as long as they do meet—which means that they must connect—real contact is established. As to the voice, changes of tone and variation of speaking pace are obviously preferable to a sleep-producing drone. Learn to assess the children's reaction to what you are saying to them, and vary your manner of speech accordingly.

Avoid pottering about the room as you are teaching, and refrain from mannerisms. In the early stages of teaching especially, it is a good idea to assume a relaxed position, perhaps seated on the front of the teacher's desk, while you are speaking, and to remain there until you must move elsewhere for a definite purpose. Remember that the blackboard, although almost the oldest visual aid, remains one of the most valuable. Use it, not only to clarify possible difficulties, but also to record the main events of your lesson. Writing and drawing on the board are skills which improve with practice. If you are not skilled in this way, get your hand in by practising. (When you do this, stand away from the board to criticize the effect of what you have done —to criticize, not to admire!) When the class is engaged upon written work, move quietly around among them, checking their efforts. This provides another means of developing an awareness of the individual child.

M.I.C.—8

Try to imagine what it must be like to be a child, of the age of those before you, sitting in one of those desks, listening to someone like yourself giving a lesson such as you are giving . . .

CONCLUSION

Lasting improvement in children's work is usually effected quite slowly. If you badger them with too many criticisms too soon you will lose their confidence and kill their enthusiasm. Remember to gauge their reactions to all you say, and to learn when they have had enough.

You will be wise to proceed very steadily at first, particularly if you find yourself teaching in a school with no previous musical activities of any merit. In such a case, be content to spend most of your first term getting the children to realize that their music lessons can be an enjoyable experience. If you conduct your first lessons with enthusiasm and a light touch, aiming primarily to build up a firm but genial relationship with the children, the chances of doing something to improve the standards of their work in the terms that follow are considerable. But if you rush in at the start, still a stranger, and persistently find fault with them, children are unlikely to give you that confidence and co-operation without which you can do very little to help them.

In your earliest contacts with a class you can afford to be much firmer with them than you intend to be when they know you better. An occasional relaxation to let them see the lighter side of your personality is a good thing. But the young teacher, unsure of his powers, who goes into his first class without letting them clearly see that he is capable of firmness as well as geniality, is making difficulties for himself, as well as encouraging the children to spend more thought on probing him for weak points than on attending to his teaching.

You can tell something of the way in which you are succeeding in your relations with schoolchildren by the way they react when they meet you in the street. If they bid you 'Good morning, sir, you score a fair average. If they cross over to the other side of the road and look in shop windows, something has gone wrong. But if they say, 'Hallo, sir,' you have arrived.

Appendix I

SOME USEFUL BOOKS

Chapter 1

Handbook for Music Teachers, London University Institute of Education (Novello)
    Includes three hundred pages of reviews of music and books recommended for school use. There are in addition forty-two articles dealing with every aspect of school music today.
Teaching Music, C. Winn (O.U.P.)
Music in the Primary School, W. Shaw (Dobson)
Music in the Secondary School, W. Shaw (Dobson)
Music in English Education, N. Long (Faber)
Music Handbook for Infant Schools, P. Pfaff (Evans)
School Music Method, R. Hunt (Ashdown)
Music in Schools, J. R. Brocklehurst (Routledge)
Teaching Music in Schools, J. Mainwaring (Paxton)
Music in Primary Schools, School Music Association
Music in Secondary Schools, School Music Association
Music in Schools, H.M.S.O.
An Outline of Musical Education, Part I, Incorporated Society of Musicians

Chapter 2

The Background of Music, H. Lowery (Hutchinson)
Music is for You, P. M. Young (Lutterworth)
Listening to Music in Schools, N. Long (Boosey)
Musical Appreciation in Schools, C. Kirkham Jones (Macmillan)
The Slow Learner and Music, J. Dobbs (O.U.P.)
Discovering Music with Young Children, E. Bailey (Methuen)
Science and Music, from Tom-tom to Hi-Fi, Berger & Clarke (Murray)
Sound Sense, G. Russell-Smith (Boosey)
Science and Music, J. Jeans (C.U.P.)
The Physics of Musical Sounds, C. A. Taylor (E.U.P.)

Chapter 3

Girls' Choirs, H. Coleman and H. West (O.U.P.)
Children Singing, C. Winn (O.U.P.)

Voice Production in Choral Technique, C. Cleall (Novello)
Youth Club Choirs, H. Coleman (O.U.P.)
Basic Choir Training, E. Wright (R.S.C.M.)

Chapter 4

Music Reading for Young Children, F. Windebank (Novello)
Sing at Sight, W. Appleby (O.U.P.)
Read & Sing, W. H. J. Jenkins (Allen & Unwin)
Read & Sing, P. Young (Allen & Unwin)
Musical Education in Hungary, F. Sandor (ed.) (Barrie & Rockliff)
Bicinia Hungarica, Z. Kodály (Boosey)
Let us Sing Correctly, Z. Kodály (Boosey)
50 Nursery Songs, Z. Kodály (Boosey)
Tunes to Read, B. Rainbow (O.U.P.)
Graded Music Reading, I. Rees-Davies (Novello)
A Music Notebook, J. N. Brown (Novello)
Elements of Music, R. Hunt (Ashdown)
Projects in Music, I. Lawrence (Longmans)
Oxford Student's Harmony, E. South and D. Renouf (O.U.P.)
Graded Music Course for Schools, A. O. Warburton (Longmans)

Chapter 5

A Natural Approach to Singing, J. Litante (O.U.P.)
Voice Training and Conducting in Schools, R. Jacques (O.U.P.)
The Art of Accompanying and Coaching, K. Adler (O.U.P.)
Practical Principles of Voice Production, Howe (Paxton)
The Boy's Changing Voice, J. P. Mellalieu (O.U.P.)

Chapter 6

Orchestral Technique, G. Jacob (O.U.P.)
Musical Instruments, A. Baines (Penguin)
Musical Instruments in the Classroom, G. Winters (Longmans)
Creative Music in Education, R. M. Thackray (Novello)
Musicianship for Guitarists, T. B. Pitfield (Mills)
The Recorder in Schools, F. Dinn (Schott)
Music for 2-part diatonic playing (Harmonica and Recorder), Rowe & Walters (Hohner)
Music through the Percussion Band, Y. Adair (Boosey)
How to Use Melodic Percussion Instruments, K. Blocksidge (Nursery Schools Association)
Making Musical Apparatus and Instruments for Use in Nursery and Infant Schools, K. Blocksidge (Nursery Schools Association)

The Auto-Harp, D. Adams-Jeremiah (Lengnick)
Hymns for School Ensemble (Harmonicas with optional violins and recorders). Two books. B. Rainbow (O.U.P.)
School Piano Class Method, R. Jevons (Jos. Williams)
Piano Class Instruction Manual, K. Axtens (Hawkes)
Music for Children, C. Orff and H. Keetman (Schott)
The School Orchestra, H. Clifford (Boosey)
School and Amateur Orchestras, J. B. Dalby (Pergamon)
The Complete Bandmaster, D. Wright (Pergamon)
Book of the School Orchestra, Newton & Young (O.U.P.)
The School Orchestra, A. Carse (Augener)
Principles of Musicianship, T. H. Yorke Trotter and S. Chapple (Bosworth)
An Introduction to String Class Teaching (Rural Schools Music Association)
Making and Playing Bamboo Pipes, M. Galloway (Dryad Press)
Musical Instruments made to be played, R. Roberts (Dryad Press)

Chapter 7

Introduction to Contemporary Music, J. Machlis (Dent)
New Sounds in Class, G. Self (Universal Edn)
20th-Century Music, R. Myers (ed.) (John Calder)
This Modern Music, G. Abraham (Duckworth)
The Composer in the Classroom, M. Schafer (Universal Edn)
A List of Contemporary Choral Music suitable for Schools, Standing Conference for Amateur Music
Experimental Music in Schools, B. Dennis (O.U.P.)

Chapter 9

Psychology for Musicians, P. Buck (O.U.P.)
Musical Ability in Children and its Measurement, A. Bentley (Harrap)
Music for the Handicapped Child, J. Alvin (O.U.P.)
Music Centres and the Training of Specially Talented Children, Standing Conference for Amateur Music

Appendix II

EXTRACT FROM A REPORT ON THE
TRAINING OF TEACHERS IN FRANCE

by BLANCHE SOURIAC, Professeur de Lycée, Paris

The most difficult thing for a young teacher giving his or her first lesson is to be perfectly natural with the children: not to imagine there is a special teacher's attitude bearing no resemblance to the real self; and, above all, to think about the children and not about oneself. In most cases our students begin by being obsessed with what they have decided to say and the course the lesson should follow at any price (their 'model' lesson) and they forget to keep their eyes on the class to see whether it is awake, attentive and interested, or whether it would not be advisable to alter the prearranged programme a little in order to arouse the interest of the audience. Yet it is only the teacher's ability to hold his pupils which makes a good class possible, and the children's sympathy must be awakened through the talent, intelligence, perhaps certain physical traits of the young teacher, and also through his character: a repressed or gloomy individual lacks the vocation for our kind of work; cheerfulness and optimism are needed to get results in our classes.

(Translated from the French)

From an address to the International Conference on the Role and Place of Music in the Education of Youth and Adults, Brussels, 1953. Published as Music in Education *(UNESCO, 1955).*

Appendix III

EXTRACT FROM A REPORT ON AIDS IN MUSIC EDUCATION

by ANTOINE E. CHERBULIEZ DE SPRECHER,
Professor, Zurich University, Switzerland

. . . the three stages of musical understanding, which every listener normally experiences.

The first of these stages consists in simple reception, which is passive, non-analytical, non-critical and even less disposed to form a synthesis. The listener makes no particular effort when hearing the music; his attention is rather vague and haphazard, and he has no really clear idea of what he is listening to. However, he grasps certain passages which please or impress him, or which seem less obscure than others . . . This is the attitude of 80 per cent of our amateur concert-goers. It is natural and even inevitable.

The second stage is the opposite of the first; it is analytical, critical, anatomical, even surgical. It is the stage at which the listener consciously decomposes the music into its different elements, in order to consider each of them separately—the technical, aesthetic and tectonic elements, artificially isolated from the work as a whole. This attitude is, no less than the first, an essential step towards musical understanding, although it has its pitfalls because it involves decomposing something that is, in fact, a composition. By splitting up the unit, by dissecting it in detail, we are subjecting an organism, into which its creator has breathed robust life, to treatment that is more applicable to dead and inorganic things.

Misfortune, therefore, awaits those who remain concentrated on analysis, who rivet their attention on technical details when listening to, or playing music.

A third stage, consequently, must be proceeded to—that in which the various elements are recomposed so as to reconstitute the work as a unit. This then is the stage of 'total conception' of the music—the stage of synthesis, a natural consequence of the analysis which has, as it were, been transcended; for in the field of music, analysis is never an end in itself.

This synthesis will enable the listener to understand music more simply and spontaneously because the work in question has been assimilated by his mind, with the help of analytical knowledge which, though it remains in the background, is none the less present and ready to aid him.

These three stages—simple reception, conscious analysis and synthesis—have their own dialectic similar to that on which Hegel's philosophy was based: thesis, antithesis, synthesis.

(Translated from the French)

From an address to the International Conference on the Role and Place of Music in the Education of Youth and Adults, Brussels, 1953. Published as Music in Education *(UNESCO, 1955).*

Appendix IV

THE FRENCH RHYTHM-NAMES

𝅝	TAA-AA-AA-AA
𝅗𝅥.	TAA-AA-AA
𝅗𝅥	TAA-AA
𝅘𝅥	TAA
𝅘𝅥𝅮𝅘𝅥𝅮	taatai
	-aatai
	saatai
	taasai
	taataitee
	taaaitee
	tafatefe

A single example should be sufficient to make clear the way in which these syllables are employed.

$\mathbf{c}$ 𝅗𝅥   𝅘𝅥   𝅘𝅥𝅮𝅘𝅥𝅮 | 𝅗𝅥.   𝅘𝅥𝅮 𝅘𝅥

   TAA-AA   TAA   taatai   TAA-aatai   TAA-AA

But remember that when the pulse value is changed, the application of the syllables changes too:

3/4 𝅗𝅥   𝅘𝅥 | 𝅗𝅥.   𝅘𝅥𝅮 𝅘𝅥 |
   TAA-AA   TAA   TAA-aatai   TAA

3/2 𝅝   𝅗𝅥 | 𝅗𝅥.   𝅘𝅥 𝅘𝅥 |
   TAA-AA   TAA   TAA-aatai   TAA

3/8 𝅘𝅥   𝅘𝅥𝅮 | 𝅘𝅥𝅮.   𝅘𝅥𝅯 𝅘𝅥𝅮 |
   TAA-AA   TAA   TAA-aatai   TAA

It is unlikely that the more complicated groupings will be employed, since this method will normally be nothing more than a preparation for staff notation. By the time children are confronted with rhythmic subtleties, their experience with staff notation will enable them to deal with the problem in that form. For that reason, only a selection of the time-names is given above.

Index

'Absolute' music 9–10
Acoustics, elementary 12
Adolescent problems 11–12
Adolescent voices 12–14, 52–54
Art teaching compared 81–83

Band and orchestra 75–78
Bobby Shaftoe set for percussion 67–69
Breathing and breath control 44–48
Broadcast lessons 94

Choral music 15–26
Clefs 36–37
Concerts for schools 97–99
Contemporary music in schools 81–90
Content of music course 5–6
Correlation with other subjects 94–95
Creative work (Percussion) 71
    „   „   (Melody-writing) 72–75

Diction 54–56
Discipline 101–106
Dotted notes 38–39

Educational value of music 3–4
Examinations 44

French Rhythm-names 30, 113

'Groaners' 62–63
Guitar tuition 77–78

Hand, singing from the, 34–36
Harmonicas 80
House Music Competitions 96–97

Instrumental tuition 75–80
Instrumental work 64–80
Integrated lessons 100–101

Key signatures 42–43

Line and phrasing 56–58
Listening to music 7–9, 91–95

Manner of the teacher 1–3, 101–106
Melody-writing 72–75
'Missing Note' Game 20

Notation 27–44

Orchestra and band 75–78
Orff, Carl 30, 64

Percussion work 64–71
Phrasing and line 56–58
Piano accompaniment 17–18
Piano-class tuition 77
Pitch-notation 32–38, 42–44
Policy-making 16–17
'Programme' music 9

Rands, Bernard 86
Recorder tuition 78–79
Recordings, private 95
Rests 39–40
Rhythmic-notation 28–32, 38–42

School Music Festivals 97
Self, George 83, 87, 88
Singing lessons 17–26
Song library 18–20
Song repertoire 61–62

Teacher's manner 1–3, 101–106
Teaching a new song 58–61
Televised lessons 94
Time signatures 40–42
Tone production 50–52
Tonic sol-fa 13, 34, 35, 89
Two-part singing 25–26

Visual response 7–8, 10–11
Vocal exercises 49–50
Vocal registers 58–50